THE
PASSION
TRANSLATION

THE PASSIONATE LIFE BIBLE STUDY SERIES

12-LESSON

T0346452

THE BOOK OF
PHILIPPIANS

heaven's joy

BroadStreet
PUBLISHING

BroadStreet Publishing® Group, LLC
Savage, Minnesota, USA
BroadStreetPublishing.com

TPT The Book of Philippians: 12-Lesson Study Guide
Copyright © 2022 BroadStreet Publishing Group

978-1-4245-6435-4 (softcover)
978-1-4245-6436-1 (e-book)

Stock or custom editions of BroadStreet Publishing titles may be purchased in bulk for educational, business, ministry, fundraising, or sales promotional use. For information, please email orders@broadstreetpublishing.com.

General editor: Brian Simmons
Managing editor: William D. Watkins
Writer: Karen Whiting

Design and typesetting by Garborg Design Works | garborgdesign.com

Printed in the United States of America

22 23 24 25 26 5 4 3 2 1

Contents

From God's Heart to Yours

"God is love," says the apostle John, and "Everyone who loves is fathered by God and experiences an intimate knowledge of him" (1 John 4:7). The life of a Christ-follower is, at its core, a life of love—God's love of us, our love of him, and our love of others and ourselves because of God's love for us.

And this divine love is reliable, trustworthy, unconditional, other-centered, majestic, forgiving, redemptive, patient, kind, and more precious than anything else we can ever receive or give. It characterizes each person of the Trinity—Father, Son, and Holy Spirit—and so is as unlimited as they are. They love one another with this eternal love, and they reach beyond themselves to us, created in their image with this love.

How do we know such incredible truths? Through the primary source of all else we know about the one God—his Word, the Bible. Of course, God reveals who he is through other sources as well, such as the natural world, miracles, our inner life, our relationships (especially with him), those who minister on his behalf, and those who proclaim him to us and others. But the fullest and most comprehensive revelation we have of God and from him is what he has given us in the thirty-nine books of the Hebrew Scriptures (the Old Testament) and the twenty-seven books of the Christian Scriptures (the New Testament). Together, these sixty-six books present a compelling and telling portrait of God and his dealings with us.

It is these Scriptures that *The Passionate Life Bible Study Series* is all about. Through these study guides, we—the editors and writers of this series—seek to provide you with a unique and welcoming opportunity to delve more deeply into God's precious Word, encountering there his loving heart for you and all the others he loves. God wants you to know him more deeply, to love him more devoutly, and to share his heart with others more frequently and freely. To accomplish this, we have based this study guide series on The Passion Translation of the Bible, which strives to "unlock the passion of [God's] heart." It is "a heart-level translation, from the passion of God's heart to the passion of your heart," created to "kindle in you a burning desire for him and his heart, while impacting the church for years to come."[1]

In each study guide, you will find an introduction to the Bible book it covers. There you will gain information about that Bible book's authorship, date of composition, first recipients, setting, purpose, central message, and key themes. Each lesson following the introduction will take a portion of that Bible book and walk you through it so you will learn its content better while experiencing and applying God's heart for your own life and encountering ways you can share his heart with others. Along the way, you will come across a number of features we have created that provide opportunities for more life application and growth in biblical understanding:

 ## Experience God's Heart

This feature focuses questions on personal application. It will help you live out God's Word, to bring the Bible into your world in fresh, exciting, and relevant ways.

 ## Share God's Heart

This feature will help you grow in your ability to share with other people what you learn and apply in a given lesson. It provides guidance on how the lesson relates to growing closer to others, to enriching your fellowship with others. It also points the way to enabling you to better listen to the stories of others so you can bridge the biblical story with their stories.

The Backstory

This feature provides ancient historical and cultural background that illuminates Bible passages and teachings. It deals with then-pertinent religious groups, communities, leaders, disputes, business trades, travel routes, customs, nations, political factions, ancient measurements and currency...in short, anything historical or cultural that will help you better understand what Scripture says and means. You may also find maps and charts that will help you reimagine these groups, places, and activities. Finally, in this feature you will find references to additional Bible texts that will further illuminate the Scripture you are studying.

 ## Word Wealth

This feature provides definitions and other illuminating information about key terms, names, and concepts, and how different ancient languages have influenced the biblical text. It also provides insight into the different literary forms in the Bible, such as prophecy, poetry, narrative history, parables, and letters, and how knowing the form of a text can help you better interpret and apply it. Finally, this feature highlights the most significant passages in a Bible book. You may be encouraged to memorize these verses or keep them before you in some way so you can actively hide God's Word in your heart.

 ## Digging Deeper

This feature explains the theological significance of a text or the controversial issues that arise and mentions resources you can use to help you arrive at your own conclusions. Another way to dig deeper into the Word is by looking into the life of a biblical character or another person from church history, showing how that man or woman incarnated a biblical truth or passage. For instance, Jonathan Edwards was well known for his missions work among native American Indians and for his intellectual prowess in articulating the Christian faith; Florence Nightingale for the reforms she brought about in healthcare; Irenaeus for his fight against heresy; Billy Graham for his work in evangelism; Moses for the strength God gave him to lead the Hebrews and receive and communicate the law; Deborah for her work as a judge in Israel. This feature introduces to you figures from the past who model what it looks like to experience God's heart and share his heart with others.

The Extra Mile

While The Passion Translation's notes are extensive, sometimes students of Scripture like to explore more on their own. In this feature, we provide you with opportunities to glean more information from a Bible dictionary, a Bible encyclopedia, a reliable Bible online tool, another ancient text, and the like. Here you will learn how you can go the extra mile on a Bible lesson. And not just in study either. Reflection, prayer, discussion, and applying a passage in new ways provide even more opportunities to go the extra mile. Here you will find questions to answer and applications to make that will require more time and energy from you—if and when you have them to give.

As you can see above, each of these features has a corresponding icon so you can quickly and easily identify them.

You will find other helps and guidance through the lessons of these study guides, including thoughtful questions, application suggestions, and spaces for you to record your own reflections, answers, and action steps. Of course, you can also write in your own journal, notebook, computer, or other resource, but we have provided you with space for your convenience.

Also, each lesson will direct you into the introductory material and numerous notes provided in The Passion Translation. There each Bible book contains a number of aids supplied to help you better grasp God's words and his incredible love, power, knowledge, plans, and so much more. We want you to get the most out of your Bible study, especially using it to draw you closer to the One who loves you most.

Finally, at the end of each lesson you'll find a section called "Talking It Out." This contains questions and exercises for application that you can share, answer, and apply with your spouse, a friend, a coworker, a Bible study group, or any other individuals or groups who would like to walk with you through this material. As Christians, we gather together to serve, study, worship, sing, evangelize, and a host of other activities. We grow together, not just on our own. This section will give you ample opportunities to engage others with the content of each lesson so you can work it out in community.

We offer all of this to support you in becoming an even more faithful and loving disciple of Jesus Christ. A disciple in the ancient world was a student of her teacher, a follower of his master. Students study and followers follow. Jesus' disciples are to sit at his feet and listen and learn and then do what he tells them and shows them to do. We have created *The Passionate Life Bible Study Series* to help you do what a disciple of Jesus is called to do.

So go.

Read God's words.

Hear what he has to say in them and through them.

Meditate on them.

Hide them in your heart.

Display their truths in your life.

Share their truths with others.

Let them ignite Jesus' passion and light in all you say and do.

Use them to help you fulfill what Jesus called his disciples to do: "Now wherever you go, make disciples of all nations, baptizing them in the name of the Father, the Son, and the Holy Spirit. And teach them to faithfully follow all that I have commanded you. And never forget that I am with you every day, even to the completion of this age" (Matthew 28:19–20).

And through all of this, let Jesus' love nourish your heart and allow that love to overflow into your relationships with others (John 15:9–13). For it was for love that Jesus came, served, died, rose from the dead, and ascended into heaven. This love he gives us. And this love he wants us to pass along to others.

Why I Love the Book of Philippians

So why do I love the book of Philippians? In one word: Joy!

Philippians is a book full of joy and rejoicing. In fact, the words *joy* and *rejoice* (rejoicing) are found nineteen times in this four-chapter book! There are nineteen reasons for joy tucked inside of Paul's letter to the Philippian believers.

What makes this letter of joy stand out is that Paul wrote it from a prison cell. That's right; he was a prisoner of the vast and powerful Roman Empire. If you were imprisoned, restricted, bound with shackles, placed in a dark dungeon cell, would you pen a letter about joy? Most of us would write an impassioned plea for prayer to relieve our suffering. Paul writes his treatise to remind every believer that "the strength of Christ's explosive power infuses me to conquer every difficulty" (Philippians 4:13).

I love the Philippians letter because it reminds me every time I open its pages to rejoice in the Lord. My momentary hardships pale in comparison to what Paul endured so that we could read this book.

Philippians is also a book of victory and overcoming hardship. The lyrics of a victory song are embedded into its four chapters. It promises to make you dance in victory to its joyful tune. Not one word of complaint is found here—only overcoming joy. Paul was misunderstood, even persecuted by other believers, yet he remained emotionally healthy enough to point us all to Jesus Christ. Paul had to endure many hardships, yet he kept his focus on Jesus Christ, the God-man of glory.

I love Philippians because great doctrines of our faith can be found in the book. We see the dual nature of Jesus as both man and God, the God-man who humbled himself and started the journey from the throne to the cross to the tomb but rose in victory to share the spoils of triumph with you and me (2:5–11).

I love Philippians because it is a book of unity and harmony, showing us how to live together in the body of Christ. Philippians teaches us how to be delivered from our unbelief and self-focus. Paul instructs us to rise above differences that would divide us as believers and to live in harmony with one another. He writes, "Be joined together in perfect unity—with one heart, one passion, and united in one love. Walk together with one harmonious purpose and you will fill my heart with unbounded joy" (2:2).

Did you know that one of the most popular verses in all the Bible is Philippians 4:6–8? Here it is:

> Don't be pulled in different directions
> or worried about a thing. Be saturated
> in prayer throughout each day, offering
> your faith-filled requests before God with
> overflowing gratitude. Tell him every detail
> of your life, then God's wonderful peace
> that transcends human understanding, will
> guard your heart and mind through Jesus
> Christ. Keep your thoughts continually fixed
> on all that is authentic and real, honorable
> and admirable, beautiful and respectful,
> pure and holy, merciful and kind. And
> fasten your thoughts on every glorious
> work of God, praising him always.

Yes, I love this book because it points me away from life's distractions and fastens my thoughts on what Jesus has done for me. Take the time to pour over this study guide and dig into the wealth of Philippians. You will find in its pages a joy unspeakable, one full of glory!

Brian Simmons
General Editor

LESSON 1

The Apostle Paul, Philippians, and Choosing Joy

Welcome to the letter to the Philippians, an epistle that flows with joy, inspires gratitude, and shares many truths about Jesus. Writing while imprisoned, Paul expresses joy and gladness nineteen times in this short book. He sees his circumstances as nothing compared to the wonder of knowing Jesus.

Philippians provides examples of Christians to imitate, delights in opportunities that even imprisonment afforded for sharing the gospel, and expresses the apostle Paul's gratitude for the support of his friends in Philippi. His perspective is not of a victim but of a thankful missionary who uses every opportunity to advance faith in Jesus and show appreciation to people who have supported him.

Ever mindful of the need for others to have faith in Jesus Christ, Paul shares a creed, also known as the *kenosis* passage or "Christ Hymn" (Philippians 2:9–11). It lays out basic facts about Christ from his preexistent glory to his sacrifice on the cross as our exalted Lord.

Paul encourages his dear friends in Philippi to live in harmony as the community of Christ. He urges these faithful followers to focus on living their faith and understanding that their true citizenship lies in heaven. This means choosing a positive attitude and finding contentment in all circumstances. Paul wants believers to look forward to the glory of God in eternity and to trust that God will strengthen them and satisfy their needs on earth. Paul also wants to inspire them to share their faith.

Authorship

Early Christians accepted that Paul wrote the book of Philippians and sent it as a letter from himself and his friend Timothy, as revealed in the letter's opening verse. The book's style and content are consistent with Paul's other known writings. Thirteen of the epistles in the New Testament are attributed to Paul, making up nearly half the total number of books in this portion of Scripture. Philippians is one of his four letters written from prison, and he wrote it to church members and leaders in Philippi, an ancient city in Macedonia. It's one of his most personal letters.

Bible scholars who focus on the New Testament letters attributed to Paul study even passages within them to determine if any are pre-Pauline texts (known to Paul but not originally composed by him) or post-Pauline (added into his letter after he wrote it, also called *interpolations*). Scholars continue to debate the original authorship of verses 2:6–11, but no one describes this passage as post-Pauline, and many scholars believe it was part of an early hymn known to Paul and thus pre-Pauline.[2] This is not the only occasion where Paul and other New Testament writers drew from outside sources.[3] But in this section of Philippians, the hymnal fragments show that the Christian belief in Jesus' exalted divine nature and status predated Paul's ministry and likely became entrenched in the church in its earliest years.

External evidence for Paul's authorship of Philippians comes from the writings of Polycarp of Smyrna (ca. 69–ca. 155), Irenaeus (ca. 120–ca. 200), Clement of Alexandria (ca. 150–215), Tertullian (ca. 155–ca. 220), and other church fathers. The internal and external evidence for Paul's authorship of this letter is so persuasive that "the vast majority of those who study the NT today are certain that Paul was responsible for Philippians."[4]

- *How do you know who really sent you an email, text, or letter? Besides the sender's name or signature, what about the writing or contents might reveal the identity of the sender?*

- *Scholars study the patterns, style, and phrases of Paul's writing to help decide if he really wrote certain epistles and passages. What's your impression of Paul's character from any of his letters you have read or studied?*

 THE EXTRA MILE

Consider Paul's tone and style. Philippians is a very personal letter and less formal than his other epistles.[5]

- *Next to each of the following passages from Paul's letters, note the reasons he gives for the letter, the tone he uses, and the way he introduces himself:*

Romans 1:1–10

1 Corinthians 1:1–13

Philippians 1:1–7

1 Timothy 1:1–7

- *What are some of the similarities you noticed?*

- *What differences did you observe?*

- *What are some different approaches you use for communicating with people?*

- *What causes you to be more serious or use a tone of reprimand?*

- *What leads you to use a warm or joyful tone?*

The Letter's Recipients

Paul addressed this letter to the church in Philippi that he started on his second missionary journey between 49 and 52 CE, detailed in Acts 16–18. He wrote the letter to be read publicly to all the believers in Philippi. Paul returned there on his third missionary trip (Acts 20:1). Generally, Paul looked for a synagogue where he could preach to Jews, but Philippi served as a Roman outpost, and too few Jews lived there to establish a synagogue (16:13). According to Jewish tradition, it took ten Jewish men to establish a synagogue.[6]

Philippi's rich history began when King Philip, the father of Alexander the Great (king of the ancient Greek kingdom or Macedon), took the town in 356 BCE, renamed it, and expanded it. The city was known for its fertile fields and nearby gold mines in the mountains to the north. In 168 BCE he captured the city. In 42 BCE, the Roman forces of Mark Antony and Octavian, loyalists to the assassinated Roman ruler Julius Caesar, defeated those of the assassins, Marcus Brutus and Gaius Cassias, outside the city of Philippi. "In celebration of the victory the city was made a Roman colony with the special privileges this involved."[7]

Many retired Roman soldiers lived in Philippi and received special privileges in exchange for helping to guard the city. About eighty years before Paul's first trip to Philippi, the Roman government granted land there to retired soldiers. Their presence added to the patriotism among the people and led to a term for the area called "The Romanness of Philippi." People prized Roman citizenship there, dressed in Roman clothing, and spoke Latin.[8] Paul's mention of his Roman citizenship and the rights that accompanied it led to his eventual release from prison in that city (16:35–40).

People Paul met in Philippi included Lydia, a merchant of purple cloth who housed him (vv. 11–15, 40); a Roman jailer, who almost committed suicide because he thought Paul and Silas had escaped after an earthquake and who ended up believing in Jesus through their ministry (vv. 25–36); and a slave girl Paul healed of demonic possession (vv. 16–18). The strange mix of people Paul encountered reflected the mix of residents in that region. In fact, the population included Thracians, Greeks, and Romans, and archaeological discoveries reveal the people's diverse religious beliefs and practices.[9]

Scholars estimate the population of Philippi during the first century at ten to fifteen thousand, with the majority of people being slaves, farmers, and service workers. Before the city became a Roman colony, its culture was Greek. As the population became more Romanized, it didn't lose its Greek roots and expressions. Even the Greek language was still used along with Latin.[10]

- *What is the mix of people in your local area? Include ethnicities, nationalities, religious perspectives, education levels, and other factors that contribute to the mix.*

- *Given the population make-up in your area, what challenges have you faced when trying to communicate or arrive at a shared understanding?*

THE BACKSTORY

Paul's first visit to Philippi marked his first time in Europe. He had planned to revisit the places he went to on his first missionary journey (15:36, 41), but an extraordinary vision from God changed his plans (16:9–12). The vision included a plea for help from a man from Macedonia, and it brought Paul to Philippi and opened the doors to start a church community there. Commenting on this event, New Testament scholar Richard Longenecker writes:

> Authentic turning points in history are few. But surely among them that of the Macedonian vision ranks high. Because of Paul's obedience at this point, the gospel went westward; and ultimately Europe and the Western world were evangelized. Christian response to the call of God is never a trivial thing. Indeed, as in this instance, great issues and untold blessings may depend on it.[11]

Silas (15:22, 40; 16:16–19) and Timothy (16:1–3) accompanied Paul on the first visit to Philippi. Luke, who was likely a resident of Philippi, also joined Paul's missionary team as indicated by the "we" language that begins in 16:10. (Luke was the writer of Acts, so by using "we," he includes himself among the travelers.)[12]

Archeology and history show that the Philippian community of Christians continued to grow after they were first established. Evidence of a Basilica to Paul with a baptistry indicate the community must have been large by the time Constantine allowed freedom of religion in 313 CE. In the second century, Polycarp wrote an epistle that spoke of the death of some Christians due to their beliefs. However, Slavic invasions at the end of the sixth century and a massive earthquake in 619 CE destroyed the city, and it never recovered.[13]

Key Themes

The main themes of Philippians are four, all centered on Jesus Christ and how to live and enjoy life his way. As one commentator points out, "The names Jesus Christ, Christ Jesus, Lord Jesus Christ, Lord Jesus, Jesus, Christ, Lord, and Savior occur 51 times in the 104 verses of the Epistle."[14]

First, there's the joyous gospel of Christ. Paul uses the word *gospel* more times in this letter than in any of his others. Along with continuing to advance the gospel among those who don't yet believe, Paul wants Christians to embrace the blessings of the gospel in their own lives. To emphasize this, he uses the words *joy* and *gladness* many times in the letter.

A second theme is Christ's lordship over everything in creation. Brian Simmons states:

> At the heart of this letter is the famed
> *Christ Hymn* (2:6–11)—a soaring melody
> of worship, adoration, and revelation of
> the majesty and superiority of Christ as
> Lord over all. This hymn expresses in lofty,
> lyrical language the story of Jesus from his
> preexistent glory to the universal praise
> of him as Lord paved by his obedience to
> death on the cross.[15]

Another theme is Christian conduct that exemplifies and honors Jesus Christ. "For Paul, such a life is a process of seizing the surpassing worth of Christ and being seized by him. It is also a progressive pursuit of Christ in which we daily die with him in order to experience the fullness of his new life."[16]

The fourth theme is living in the community of Christ. We are citizens of heaven no matter our earthly citizenship, and as such we need to submit to Christ's lordship. And since we are all his, we should live as family members in God's household.

- *Of these four themes, which one(s) interests you the most and why?*

- *What do you hope to gain by studying Philippians?*

 EXPERIENCE GOD'S HEART

Through this letter we are called to rejoice and understand basic truths about Christ. Consider what role joy plays in your life.

- *What opportunities do you have to share your joy and faith with family, neighbors, friends, or coworkers?*

- *What helps you remain joyful when you face struggles?*

- *How do examples of joyful Christians encourage and motivate you? What about their joy impresses you most and why?*

💙 SHARE GOD'S HEART

Paul reveals his zeal for God through his appreciation of the opportunity to witness while imprisoned, and he shows the importance of the community of believers in his appreciation of the people in Philippi and his encouragement for them to live in harmony. Like Paul, the joy that remains in you always will be a great witness to people who struggle with the worries of their circumstances.

- *Do you know people who are facing hardship and need joy? What can you say to them to bring them hope and lift their spirits?*

- *Share how your change in perspective about a struggle impacted people around you.*

Talking It Out

Since Christians grow in community, not just in solitude, here are some questions you may want to discuss with another person or in a group. Each "Talking It Out" section is designed with this purpose in mind.

1. Paul wrote letters to stay connected with other Christians. How have you stayed connected to Christians who moved away? How does staying connected differ depending on the relationship you have (mentor, mentee, fellow laborer)?

2. The unity of believers is important in faith communities. It's also one of the themes in Philippians. What helps you maintain harmony with fellow Christians in spite of any differences of belief or practice you may have?

3. Another theme is joy. How do you define joy? When troubles come or people around you argue and grumble, how do you maintain joy? What more do you hope to learn about joy in Philippians?

LESSON 2

Great Joy

(1:1–11)

Can you remember a time when friends brought smiles and laughter when you most needed it? When has someone blessed you with an action or gift that filled your heart with thanks? Those are precious blessings that delight us and lead us to be grateful.

Paul begins this letter with deep and abiding gratitude for his friends in Philippi. He pours out a heartfelt prayer for God to bless their lives and shares how he remains joyful in spite of difficult circumstances. This letter reveals his deep love for the Philippian believers.

Long before scientific studies explained the benefits of gratitude,[17] Paul's example showed how gratitude leads to an optimistic perspective. Paul shares how he views the negative circumstances as great opportunities to share the gospel. His example helps us reframe our problems into new possibilities.

Tone of the Letter

The opening words of chapter one set the tone for the letter. This is not one where Paul needs to correct the readers' beliefs or behavior. This letter exudes joy and thanks. In Acts 16:11–40, the Philippians had experienced the shock of Paul and Silas being imprisoned and beaten soon after they met. The authorities threw them in jail in Philippi, and there Paul and Silas sang songs of joy and praise. An earthquake freed them from the chains and provided an opportunity to witness to their jailor. After their release, Paul and Silas met with the city's believers, who received comfort and encouragement from them, learning, no doubt, what it means to experience joy in difficult circumstances and how even imprisonment can lead to spreading the gospel.

Not all Paul's letters use this affectionate tone.

- *Read Galatians 1:6 and 3:1. Contrast Paul's tone there with the one expressed in Philippians 1:1–8.*

- *What do the differences suggest about the situations that led Paul to write each letter?*

Greetings

Paul and Timothy

The opening greeting of Philippians 1:1 shares who wrote this letter and who its first recipients were. Then Paul labels Timothy and himself "servants of Jesus." The Greek word Paul uses for "servant" is *doulos*, which means a slave or someone who belongs totally to another person, their master.[18] In ancient Rome, some slaves were forced to work without wages, and the individual had no life of his own. Other slaves, however, received wages and rewards for work well done and could even be freed by their master. Moreover, while some slaves' lives were hard and short, "many slaves were educated, practicing as doctors, architects and teachers, and some amassed large fortunes."[19] When Paul used the term *doulos* to refer to himself and Timothy, he identified their master to be Jesus—hardly a harsh and demanding slave owner. Paul's point was that they were completely and freely dedicated to serving the all-loving and all-good Lord.

- *Why would being a slave to Jesus be a positive identity?*

- *How would you describe your relationship to Christ?*

Jesus

Jesus is called the Anointed One, the *Christos* in Greek. The word translated "Anointed One" also means Messiah. We now use Christ as a name, but the early church used it as a title that reflected the divinity of Jesus. Anointing refers to smearing or pouring oil on the head. The Hebrew prophets anointed kings with a ceremony to set the person apart as a ruler under God (1 Samuel 9:25–10:1; 1 Kings 1:32–40; 1 Chronicles 29:22–27). Priests were also anointed (Exodus 30:30; Leviticus 8:12).

• *What titles and terms do you use to describe Jesus and why?*

• *Read Acts 10:38. What is the importance of being anointed?*

THE BACKSTORY

In biblical times, shepherds poured oil on the heads of their sheep to kill lice and other insects that could kill the sheep by burrowing deep into the animal's skin or ears. The oil made it too slippery for the insects to crawl. Anointing became a symbol of protection and blessing and fits well with Jesus as the Anointed One, who is also called the Good Shepherd.[20]

The Philippian Church

Paul calls the church members "devoted followers." The Greek in Philippians 1:1 translates the word for "devoted" as "guardians," while the Aramaic translation is "priests."[21] *Guardian* implies they are engaged and loyal to their faith and protect the teachings about Christ. In the Old Testament, God established priests to oversee the sacrifices and offerings (Leviticus 6:8–7:36). They had other responsibilities as well, including keeping the Bread of Presence on the table in the tent of meeting, keeping the tabernacle lamps burning, overseeing the feasts of Israel, and mediating between God and the Hebrews. In essence, they maintained the relationship between God and the people of Israel.

Paul wanted believers to handle God's Word correctly (2 Timothy 2:15). The greeting also reminds people to be devoted in their roles.

- *How are you devoted as a believer and a guardian of the Word?*

- *What does it mean to you to handle God's Word carefully? What helps you remain accurate and true to the Scriptures?*

The Church's Leaders

Paul refers to the leaders as "servant-leaders" (Philippians 1:1). The original wording in Greek, *dia kovis*, can also be translated "deacon," "servant," or "minister."[22] The term means "to kick up the dust and be swift." That referenced the ability to work fast, stirring up the dust in the street while running.[23] The same zeal Paul had, he wanted to see in others who serve the Lord, to see their passion and hard work.

- *Knowing Paul wants workers to be passionate, what work do you do that shows your passion for Christ and lets others see your zeal for your faith?*

- *What focus and passion do you see in your Christian leaders? What kind of zeal do you wish church leaders would demonstrate? How does passion for Christ in others inspire you?*

Teens may not do well in school and feel disconnected with the subject material. Once a student develops a passion and decides on a career, that teen will focus and do well in school. They become devoted students. That's also true in our faith. Once we encounter Christ personally and develop a passion for our faith, we focus and devote ourselves to the Word. Our passion helps us become more effective as faith leaders and followers. We kick up the dust in our zeal for God.

- *How does passion and devotion to Christ help your focus in your chosen vocation?*

- *How does it help you work more effectively?*

- *How can you stay connected with Christ, and how will that help you stay passionate about your faith?*

Blessings

Paul has been called the Apostle of Grace. In Philippians 1:2, Paul calls for a blessing of divine grace and supernatural peace to the recipients. He uses the greeting of grace and peace in each of his letters and closes each with the desire for God's grace to be with the recipients. Grace used here is the Greek word *charis*. It is also translated as "kindness."

God's grace played a vital role in Paul's life and conversion.

- *Look up the following verses and note what Paul wrote about grace in each one:*

  Romans 15:15–16

  1 Corinthians 15:10

  2 Corinthians 1:12

  2 Corinthians 12:9–10

  Galatians 1:15–16

  Ephesians 3:7–8

- *How has God's grace impacted your life?*

Peace

Peace is the other word Paul uses in greetings, and it comes after *grace* (Philippians 1:2). It's hard to have peace without God's grace. Through grace, Paul changed from an angry man intent on wiping out the followers of Christ and discovered love when Christ met him on the road to Damascus.

- *Review the story in Acts 9:1–22 and write notes about Paul's anger and attitude before he met Christ.*

Paul uses the phrase "supernatural peace" that flows from God and Jesus, the Messiah. The Greek word used in Philippians 1:2 and in 4:7, *eirene,* is also translated as "rest and quietness." [24] The second passage mentioned expands this peace by describing it as "peace that transcends human understanding" and states it "will guard your heart and mind through Jesus Christ." This is a peace that keeps away the worry and anxiety that disrupts the mind; it's an inner peace. This is the blessing of peace Paul wanted for the Philippians.

- *Paul was at peace even in prison and attributed it to grace. How does God's grace help you have inner peace?*

- *How has God blessed you with peace in difficult situations?*

Paul's Prayer

Read Philippians 1:3–11. Paul's prayer is full of joy and hope as he praises God for his friends. He expresses love and affection for them. Gratitude is the reason for his joy. Look at his use of the superlatives *full* and *great*. This shows his strong appreciation for the Philippian believers.

In note 'd' for verse 6, we find a comparison between the good work begun in the Philippians with the good work of creation that God performed in Genesis 1. God sees our growth in grace and the new creation life within us as something good. In 2 Corinthians 5:17, Paul states that believers are new persons. Just as God saw that the earth he created and all that is in it was good, so Paul uses the term *good work* regarding believers, a work that God will continue to nurture into maturity.

- *When have you been thankful for growth that God caused? Describe what happened.*

- *Which believers give you joy? Why?*

- *Sometimes people help us grow stronger in our relationship with Christ. How does knowing people who bring you joy also bring you closer to God?*

- *In Philippians 1:1–11, what does Paul say that indicates his desire for his friends as far as their growth, spiritual insight, and choices?*

Results of Choosing the Excellent Way

Verses 9–11 focus on making excellent choices that lead to righteousness and bring glory and praise to God. Paul starts this section by admonishing his readers to love others, and then he moves to the matter of discerning how to live a pure and holy (blameless) life. When we love others, we make choices that will not offend or hurt them. When we love God, we make choices to live to please him and thus take time to see if our choices measure up to his standards. The word translated "pure" is *eilikrines*, meaning "unmixed or without alloy."[25] It's a choice to be sincere and authentic.

Discernment helps us choose how to conduct ourselves in ways that build character. People watch us to see how we live, and that becomes a witness to God. The fruits of righteousness mentioned in verse 11 are the evidence of our godly choices.

- *What are some key biblical passages that help guide you to make good choices?*

- *Read the following passages, and list how they can help you in your decision making:*

   1 Kings 3:9

   Proverbs 18:15

   Micah 6:8

   James 3:17–18

   1 John 4:1–3

God views the growth of Christians as good and worthwhile. The ultimate goal of their choices and growth, stated in Philippians 1:11, is to bring praise and glory to God.

The Process of Maturity

Paul shares his confidence in Philippians 1:7 that Christ will continue to mature them. This is a process and not an instant result of becoming a Christian or reading the Bible once. It takes time for a baby to grow, develop, and mature—physically and mentally. New Christians are spiritual babies who need to develop gradually. Paul connects the maturity to the gracious (full of grace) work

God has begun. It's God working in us. Grace causes the growth and the change. The believers' response is to be faithful, to be open to God's work within us.

• *How has God's grace changed you?*

• *Do you know any Christians who seem mature in their faith? What are the signs of maturity that you have seen in them?*

Themes Introduced

In the first verses of Paul's letter, he introduces a few topics and alludes to others. We discover the epistle's major themes as he shares his desires for the Philippian Christians. One of these desires is community.

- *How does Paul describe his letter's recipients in verses 3–4 and 7?*

- *What are Paul's sentiments toward his readers?*

- *How do his words help build community?*

- *How can we partner with fellow Christians to build community?*

In verses 3–4, Paul also introduces the word *joy*, another theme of the letter. His joy flows from the support of the community.

- *What expectations or hopes can you identify for yourself before you continue reading this letter?*

Sharing Christ

Paul brought up Christ as the Anointed One as well as Jesus' unveiling, the future knowledge we will have about him. These believers already had faith in Christ, but Paul knew that they could learn still more about him. The apostle will continue to share about Christ in the letter, including his lordship, and his example to help their faith grow.

• *What is something new you've learned about Christ recently?*

 EXPERIENCE GOD'S HEART

Imprisonment during Paul's time meant great hardship. Paul could have felt sorry for himself, but he chose joy. He said in verse 3, "My prayers for you are full of praise to God as I give him thanks for you with great joy."

• *Let people know they have given you reasons to choose joy. You can say this to them, write a note to them, or express it in other ways. Like Paul, be encouraging to those who have uplifted your spirit.*

SHARE GOD'S HEART

Philippians 1:6 communicates Paul's joy in seeing people he discipled continue to grow in faith. That enabled Paul to pray with great faith. Knowing God continues to work and mature us should bring great hope. Knowing we have a community of believers should bring great joy.

- *How does seeing God continue to work in your life and the lives of others give you the courage to share your faith?*

- *Paul prayed with confidence. What does that mean to you? What is your favorite way to pray?*

- *What inspires you to offer to pray with someone?*

Talking It Out

1. Describe what you felt like when you first realized you were a new creation? How have you grown in faith, and what helps you mature spiritually?

2. The Greek word translated "unveiling" in Philippians 1:10 is *emeran*, meaning "day." Many translations say "until the day of the Lord" or "the day of Christ." The day of the Lord refers to a time in the future when Jesus will return. His appearance will also be a time of revealing or unveiling. How do such phrases and thoughts bring you hope or excitement about that time?

3. Paul calls the Philippians "partners" in the gospel. How are we also partners in the gospel? What can you do this week to partner in the good news about Christ? Write it down and follow through.

4. Paul shares basic truths about Jesus in chapter two. Share some of the truths that you know about Jesus and explain why they are important.

LESSON 3

Opportunities and Warnings

(1:12–26)

The COVID-19 pandemic of 2020 brought isolation to many people, especially the elderly. It's not easy to be unable to meet with people or hug them. Struggles, hard times, and even isolation from friends and family happen. How we respond is what makes the difference in our lives and how we impact the lives of those around us. We can choose to find joy in our situation, hold a pity party, or become depressed.

Joy underscores all that Paul writes as he shares how prison allowed him to witness to Roman guards and government officials and use his circumstances to embolden other believers. Paul's focus in his letter turns to his perspective on his imprisonment, warnings about motives, and the real goal of sharing Christ.

The Right Perspective

- *Read Philippians 1:12–14 and note every good that came from Paul's imprisonment. Fill in the chart of the benefits that came.*

To What or Who	Benefits
Paul's ministry	
Roman guards and government officials	
Believers	

According to Warren W. Wiersbe, "Paul's chains gave him contact with the lost. He was chained to a Roman soldier twenty-four hours a day. These shifts changed every four hours, which meant Paul could witness to at least four men each day."[26] His chains, instead of being just signs of bondage and captivity, became links to new connections.

- *Read Romans 8:28. How have your negative circumstances or problems resulted in unexpected blessings and opportunities?*

Good news can come from prison too. The Religious News Service story "Seminaries Partner with Prisons to Offer Inmates New Life as Ministers" shared how prisoners are becoming field ministers. These inmates with life or long-term sentences receive free degrees in return for a commitment to minister to other inmates. One student, James Benoy said, "It's transformed us. We have a purpose, a direction, and a mission in life."[27] Prison can transform lives and bring opportunity to share the gospel, especially with a positive attitude and the right motives.

- *When have you been blessed or have found new opportunities when you kept a positive perspective during a challenging time?*

Motives for Preaching

Motives are the underlying reasons for our actions or what inspires us to do something. The best motive for any action Christians undertake is to glorify God and spread the gospel message. Our deeds are not a measure of motives; otherwise, Christ would have highly praised the Pharisees for their outward observances of the Law. Jesus recognized their deeds as outward displays to garner attention and inwardly done for selfish gain, including power. He called them hypocrites. Years later, Paul similarly saw people's good and bad motives for preaching about Christ.

- *Read Philippians 1:15–18 where Paul describes some people preaching about Christ with impure motives. What were their wrong reasons for preaching?*

- *What have you noted happens when you or people around you allow jealousy to fester?*

- *On the other hand, what happens when you view the success of someone with grace and love?*

- *Often the easiest way to overcome feelings of jealousy is to pray for the person you envy. Try it this week. Think of one person about whom you've harbored jealousy and pray daily for God to bless that person and help you to love him or her. Note how you feel at the end of the week.*

Pure Motives

The preachers who knew that Paul was destined for a great purpose had purer motives. They understood his calling to defend the faith (apologetics) and that he acted out of love. Paul wanted to please God and not people. Likewise, Jesus came to glorify God as seen in his words in John 12:27–28. Jesus remained God focused, prayer focused, and full of love and gratitude. Those actions help keep our motives pure.

- *Read Romans 12:3–8 about working as the body of Christ. How might realizing that we are each called to different roles for a different purpose keep you from jealousy and help you rejoice at the success of others?*

Ambition and Competition versus Trusting God

Read Philippians 1:17–18. Some people seem to be born competitors. They boast and bring up comparisons when they do well. Paul says that people who "preach Christ with ambition and competition" have mixed motives. They're preaching, not so much to share the good news about Christ, but to win the attention of others, to be seen as the best gospel presenters, even outdoing Paul.

This competitive approach happens in almost any area of life from how our children are doing to our work, sports, and even cooking. We want to serve, but we also want to be praised. We have a hard time not comparing ourselves with others.

- *When has someone's boasting made you feel insignificant?*

- *Can you recall a time when you boasted to win the approval of others? What happened?*

- *How can boasting and someone else's ambition cause problems for you and others?*

The Bottom Line

Paul looked at the bottom line, the results. He rejoiced even when people had wrong motives. He finds joy that the gospel is being preached. He looks beyond motives to God's goal. That doesn't mean the person's actions or motives have God's approval. Paul's purpose is to show how we can look at what's happening through God's eyes and find the good that can occur no matter what people intend for themselves.

Roman society honored competition. And Jewish teachers believed that it was better to serve God from impure motives than not to serve at all. However, they also insisted "that those who used the law only for their own gain would not share in the world to come."[28]

It can be hard for pastors to not compete with fellow ministers. For instance, pastors with large congregations must resist boasting and feeling pride over the number of people in their pews. Those with small congregations must focus on their own calling and the resulting blessings of their work. The same is true for all of us in our own life and work.

- *Read Acts 20:22–24. What did Paul consider more important than his life?*

- *What is your life focus, and does it help you think beyond yourself to others?*

- *Are you able to resist comparing yourself to others and to their successes? If so, what helps you? If not, what stands in your way?*

- *When you have success, how can you share it to encourage people without causing jealousy or being boastful?*

- *Those preaching out of selfish motives are insincere but still sharing God's Word, so Paul still rejoices. He doesn't indicate that these people are preaching false doctrine. How is this preaching different from what Paul condemns in Galatians 1:6–9?*

 WORD WEALTH

Thlipsin is a Greek word Paul uses in Philippians 1:17. It means "tribulation" and is also translated as "hardship, trouble, or distress." Stressors cause stress, and the stressors can be circumstances or people that make things more difficult. We can crack under the stress that causes anxiety or depression.

Or we can let stress motivate us. That's called *eustress*, such as the stress of thirst motivating us to get a drink of water. It's viewing the problem as a challenge to do something positive or to react by choosing a positive attitude rather than letting the circumstances overwhelm us.

- *What are your stressors?*

- *What helps you reframe stress into a challenge (a eustress)?*

Shameless Paul

Paul declares in Philippians 1:19–21 that he will not be ashamed. He is speaking about his friends praying for him while he is in jail and waiting his trial. In verse 20 Paul states he desires Christ to be revealed to everyone through him. He views a trial as a great opportunity to witness about Christ and spread the gospel.

• *What people might have heard Paul speak at a trial?*

• *Read Romans 1:16–18 and list reasons Paul was not ashamed to preach Christ.*

• *In Mark 13:11, what did Jesus tell his followers about what to say when they are brought to trial?*

- *Bible scholars believe that Paul wrote Ephesians the same year that he penned Philippians. Read Ephesians 6:19. What was Paul's prayer request?*

- *Read Colossians 4:3–4. What was a benefit of imprisonment for Paul?*

The End Goal: Magnifying Christ

Paul also states his desire that Christ is magnified in him (Philippians 1:20). The Greek word used is *megalunthesetai*. It means "to make or declare great" and is translated as "enlarged," "exalted," "magnified," or "to get glory."[29] To magnify Christ has been compared to using a telescope that brings the stars closer and provides clarity. The unsaved see Jesus magnified and brought closer when they watch believers go through a crisis.[30]

- *How does the desire to magnify Christ make it easier to face trials and suffering?*

- *Read John 3:25–32. What did John the Baptist preach about Christ that shows his perspective of his own importance and life in respect to Jesus?*

To Live or Die

Shakespeare's play *Hamlet* includes often quoted lines that reflect man's struggle about existence: "To be or not to be, that is the question." Paul reflects on the same question but with the perspective of knowing that human death for believers brings us into the presence of God. In Philippians 1:20–24, Paul shares his thoughts about life and death and that he is torn between the two.

- *What thoughts strike you most in these verses?*
-

- *What is the purpose of Paul's life?*

- *What is the purpose of your life?*

How Do We Live Christ?

Paul states, "My true life is the Anointed One and dying means gaining more of him" (v. 21). In many other translations (KJV, NASB, NIV, NKJV, for example), this verse reads, "To live is Christ, and to die is gain." In a nutshell, Paul lived to know Christ better, to follow his example, and to point others to Christ. He lived focused on Christ and eternity. Read each of the following passages about living for Christ and write your thoughts about each text.

- *1 Corinthians 9:23*

- *Galatians 2:20*

Paul's Dilemma

Paul wrote about the consequences of living or dying. He looked at the benefit to the people he discipled and the personal benefit if he died. He found purpose for his life either way. (Note: There's a link between lack of purpose and mental illness, so be sure you are aware of that connection and how to know if someone's talk about life and death is healthy or suicidal.)

• *Read Philippians 1:21–25 and list the benefits Paul noted for living and for dying.*

• *Have you considered the shortness of your own life? If so, what significant choices have you made on how to live?*

- *How do you continue to live based on the reality and power of the gospel?*

The Power of Unity

Paul ends the chapter with a message of unity as well as encouragement for courage in suffering for Christ. He knew the strength that the support and prayers of his friends gave him. He wants them to stand united so they will share that same strength from unity in the face of any suffering.

- *Read Philippians 1:27–30. Consider what you have found in life that compares to what Paul shares about unity in each of these aspects:*

  Celebrating together

  Conquerors

  Unshaken faith that is not intimidated by opposition

  Endurance in suffering

To Paul, the people praying were striving with him. They were part of a team working toward a common goal regardless of the challenges they may face.

- *How is prayer a way of walking beside another person?*

- *How do we join in unity of purpose as we pray for someone?*

Suffering

In writing about striving together, Paul also brought up the unspoken fear of persecution. The Philippians knew about Paul's beatings and imprisonment. Paul shared how to live for Christ and keep focused on the hope of being with Christ for eternity. Paul's example showed them the courage to endure conflict and reframe it as challenges for new opportunities.

Suffering is a hard topic for many people who pray for healing and removal of problems. Christian scholar Dallas Willard wrote concerning the cost of discipleship that "suffering for him [Christ] is actually something we rejoice to be counted worthy of (Acts 5:41, Philippians 1:29). The point is simply that unless we clearly see the superiority of what we receive as his students over every other thing that might be valued, we cannot succeed in our discipleship to him."[31]

- *How have you or others you know endured real suffering? Share how any of those times opened opportunities to share the faith.*

- *Have you or people you know endured suffering on account of faith in Christ? Describe what happened and how hope helped.*

The Joyous Perspective

What does it take to have joy always? Paul shares some great secrets. We've looked at his gratitude and positive outlook. His personal mission statement is Philippians 1:21. As it was for Paul, Christ should be the beginning, middle, and end for us daily.

Paul has a few boundaries that hedge his joy:

> Live with no actions or choices that bring shame.
>
> Face life with courage by focusing on Jesus and eternity.
>
> Know that life will get better with Christ, especially our forever life.

- *Do you have any boundaries that hedge your joy? If so, what are they?*

- *What will you gain by going to heaven?*

- *Jesus said to Pilate, "You would have no power over me at all, unless it was given to you from above" (see John 19:8–11). How do Jesus' words to Pilate give you courage in anticipation of persecution? Have you seen your response of joy work to deter someone who is trying to bully or persecute you?*

🖤 EXPERIENCE GOD'S HEART

Paul shared his confidence that his time in prison would end in his freedom, and it eventually did. He viewed his incarceration as time to add to the joy of his friends and more time to help them mature in their faith.

Most of us will never experience jail time and the anguish that can come with it. But other life experiences can lead to suffering too. Consider terminal illness, for example. Even that can be faced through the eyes and strength of our faith in Christ. As one woman wrote:

> My husband and I responded to the
> possibilities of his cancer diagnoses with
> three possible outcomes of death, cure,
> or possibly living a life filled with pain

and possibly a vegetative state. We knew we could accept any of those, so cancer had no fear over us. He lived a number of years and worked and shared his faith except for the final month of his life. Even then, he enjoyed visits from family and friends and had no pain. Neighbors often mentioned that they saw our faith in how we lived. People notice how we react to life and death situations, and we can inspire them when we face those days unafraid. My husband spent time on his last day, as always, putting others first. That included leaving little gifts for me that he hid among his possessions and dictated final messages of encouragement to our children.[32]

How can a person rejoice all the time? How can someone smile when their heart is breaking? For Paul, the answer included keeping his focus on Jesus, cultivating a thankful heart, and discovering ways to continue with his call to spread the gospel despite his circumstances. Paul shows us how to choose joy. We cannot control how others treat us or even when and how death may come, but we can choose how to respond.

- *How will you respond to your circumstances and choose joy this week?*

SHARE GOD'S HEART

Paul's courage inspired many people in his day and for centuries since then. Fear is a big reason people don't share their faith. Yet, we do like to share good news and what's new with us or loved ones. That's the time to also share faith or to add how God answered a prayer, blessed you, or gave you the strength you needed. You can even open a conversation with those little nuggets. It can be very simple, such as responding to "God bless you" when you sneeze with "He has, and I pray God will also bless you."

- *Whom do you know who might need to hear how you found joy while facing hardship? Look for opportunities to share with this person your experience with God and the joy you have in him.*

THE BACKSTORY

Many scholars believe Paul's imprisonment in Philippians took place in Rome due to his mention of the Roman guards. Some scholars, however, think he could have been imprisoned in the praetorium in Caesarea.

Acts 28 indicates Paul spent two years under house arrest in Rome, and that may be when he wrote to the Philippians. Acts 28:16 says that a soldier guarded him, but he could live anywhere and had to provide for his own expenses, including meals.

- *Check out these various passages that mention Paul's imprisonments and jot down some notes on what you learn about Paul, his situation, and how he regarded it:*

Acts 28:17, 23, 31

Ephesians 6:18–20

Colossians 4:2–4

2 Corinthians 6:5; 11:23

Acts 23:35

DIGGING DEEPER

Archeological digs uncovered one of the harshest Roman prisons during Paul's time. The *Carcer Tullianum* ("The Tullianum Prison" in Latin), also called "Mamertine Prison," was located between the bottom of the Capitoline Hill and the entrance way of the Forum. The building began as a cultic center around an artificial dugout spring that still gushes water. Romans used it as a holding cell for people they considered high-value captives. By the seventh century, the jail became a holy site, revered, as tradition had it, as the place where Romans imprisoned Paul and Peter although evidence does not support that tradition. The historian Sallust's description included "a hideous and terrifying appearance."[33]

 THE EXTRA MILE

Paul was not the first faithful follower to trust in God during his prison circumstance. Read about each of the following men held in captivity and how they responded.

Person	Circumstances	Person's Response	Lesson for Me
Joseph Genesis 39:19; 40; 41:8–14; 50:15–20			
Jeremiah Jeremiah 32:2–12			

Daniel Daniel 1			
John the Baptist Matthew 14:3–12; Luke 3:20; John 3:30			
Peter Acts 12:1–4			

 THE BACKSTORY

According to history, Paul was released from his imprisonment and later arrested again and imprisoned in Rome. The fourth century church father Jerome wrote that Paul was beheaded under the emperor Nero at Rome on the same day as Peter's martyrdom. And like Peter, Paul was executed "for Christ's sake...the twenty-seventh year after our Lord's passion."[34] This would place the executions in the year 67 CE.

Talking It Out

1. We sometimes live with invisible chains from fear. What chains of fear have you carried in your life? How did you (or can you) be free from those chains?

2. Paul ends the chapter stating that he is not giving up. What in your life motivates you to press forward and not give up?

3. Whom do you know who really needs Jesus? How will you share your faith with that person?

LESSON 4

United in Love

(2:1–11)

A young priest received his first assignment to be a chaplain in an asylum. He sat beside one patient who was a former nun, not knowing she hated clergy and purposely did things to upset the chaplains when they visited. As he started to speak to her, she turned and vomited on him. He slowly pulled out his handkerchief, unfolded it, and then began wiping off her face. A tear slid down her cheek, and that began her healing. She later said that was the first time in her life that anyone put her first. The priest believed we are all united through Christ and must show God's love to everyone. He exemplified the spirit of the first part of Philippians chapter two.[35]

When we truly experience the tender mercy of the Holy Spirit and overflow with comforting love, then we willingly share that love.

Encouraged through Knowing Christ

Read Philippians 2:1. Notice the great benefits of a relationship with the triune God. The description reflects a God who wants a personal relationship with each believer, One who continually gives to an experiential relationship. The word *friendship* (with the Holy Spirit) comes from the Greek word *koinonia*, which means "fellowship." It's related to the word *koinonos* that means "companion, fellowship, or partner."[36] The origin of *companion* is Latin and means "to break bread with." This type of relationship with the Holy Spirit indicates that it's a close, intimate one.

- *Describe your friendship with the Holy Spirit (or desire for a close friendship).*

- *List the phrases in verses 1–2 that describe a deep relationship with Christ, the Anointed One.*

Call to Unity

In verses 2–3, Paul continues his encouragement for his friends to be united.

- *What are the four characteristics of unity that he desires for them?*

Paul says that this kind of unity will fill his heart with extravagant, unlimited joy. On the other hand, discord brings strife and a clash of wills. Paul wants to see among the Philippian believers the depth of harmony that brings peace.

Love is the glue that bonds people in unity. When we love others, we want the best for them, and we do not compare people or envy the blessings of others. We accept each one and see, through God's eyes, what is loveable about each individual. Walking together with the same purpose unites us as partners on the same team.

- *How is unity a choice to join together?*

• *What passions do you share within the body of believers?*

• *How can your relationship with Christ and friendship with the Holy Spirit help you live in harmony with other believers?*

Selflessness

Loving caregivers are usually selfless people. They know the person in need can give little in return. They give up their own desires and sacrifice their time to bring comfort and to provide needed care to others. This sometimes means putting dreams and careers on hold indefinitely.

Like Paul, Christians with pure motives are willing to make personal sacrifices in order to spread the gospel. They forget about self-promotion in order to bring everlasting joy to others. Paul understood the heart of being joined to Christ that led to being selfless.

Read verses 3–5. Pride, self-promotion, and selfishness are all counter to unity. The culmination of being able to achieve unity is having the mindset of Christ.

- *Why does Paul urge people to be free of pride-filled opinion?*

- *When have you seen division because of opinions tied to pride?*

- *When have you felt driven to do something that put yourself first? What helped you reevaluate?*

Self-promotion often stems from feeling inadequate or unaccepted. With unity and shared goals, we encourage and accept one another. We become a team and more easily put others first. That also means noticing the needs of others and those who seem desperate because of great needs.

- *What matters to your loved ones or friends or work associates, and how can you put them first and offer them encouragement?*

- *How would you describe the mindset of Christ?*

- *How have you let that mindset motivate you?*

The Example of Christ

Read Philippians 2:7–11. This section shares basic doctrines about Jesus Christ. Many theologians consider this Christological declaration to be an early creed or hymn that Paul used, so it may predate even Paul's conversion and ministry. In Greek, this passage is written in poetic form in couplets. Paul used it to encourage others as he shared the selflessness of Christ.[37]

In The Passion Translation (TPT), study note 'f' on Philippians 2:8 explains that verses 7–11 mention seven steps Christ took to his ultimate sacrifice on the cross: (1) he emptied himself; (2) he became a servant; (3) he became human; (4) he humbled himself; (5) he became vulnerable and was revealed as a man; (6) he was obedient even to his death; and (7) he died a criminal's death on the cross. These steps reveal a progression of intensity in the humiliation and suffering of Christ. Let's consider each of them, for they present essential truths, core beliefs, about Jesus Christ.

1. Jesus emptied himself of outward glory when he became human. His human conception is unlike any other. This is called *kenosis*. The eternal Son of God, without sacrificing his divine nature, surrendered his outward glory as he came down from his heavenly throne. In John 17:5, Jesus asks the heavenly Father to glorify him so he will again have the glory he had before the world began. His willingness to be poured out and to sacrifice his glory is a great contrast to the pride of humans mentioned in Philippians 2:3–4.

2. Jesus became a servant who washed the feet of his disciples (John 13:1–17). He did not lord his deity over others. Instead he served those he created. That is not the normal way of any earthly master or leader.

3. Jesus became human and took on the form of a man, bearing humanity's weaknesses, yet without sin. In John 1:1 we read that the Word, or Logos, was in the beginning and was with God and was God. In human history, the Logos

then became flesh (v. 14) and lived among us as one of us. Hebrews 4:15 reminds us that this Logos, Jesus the Christ, the very Son of God, experienced what humans experience. He was tempted, grew thirsty and hungry, wept, became tired, showed anger in the temple, traveled on foot, and did innumerable other things that revealed his humanity.

4. Jesus humbled himself. He even allowed himself to be tried by Jewish and Roman officials, to suffer physical beatings, and to be nailed to a cross and executed with criminals. He knew that one of his own followers, Judas, would betray him for the price of a slave, and he did not try to stop him. In short, Jesus gave up his heavenly, godly privileges, and lived and died as a human being, serving other men, women, and children.

5. Jesus became vulnerable and was revealed as a man. Other translations say he was found in the appearance as a man. Once Jesus began his ministry, demons recognized him, and religious leaders tried to trap him to undermine his ministry and teaching and find legitimacy for arresting him and killing him. Jesus' miracles exposed his power and divine favor. And his great wisdom frustrated and thwarted various leaders while amazing the common people who heard him. As great as he was, he remained vulnerable to death as all human beings are.

6. He was obedient unto death. The Authority of authorities submitted himself to the authority of his parents (Luke 2:51). He followed the Jewish laws and customs, and he obeyed God's commands in the Hebrew Scriptures. Jesus was so obedient that he could say of himself, "I do nothing on my own initiative, but I only speak the truth that the Father has revealed to me" (John 8:28). And this he did, all the way to the grave.

7. He died a criminal's death on the cross. Only a few people recognized the true identity of Jesus as he hung on the

cross, and one of those was a criminal hanging next to him. He asked Jesus to remember him when Jesus came into his kingdom, and Jesus replied to him, "I promise you—this very day you will enter paradise with me" (Luke 23:43). In Roman days, the cross represented torture and death. It was a cruel form of public humiliation, especially used to punish political and religious agitators.

- *Which of these seven steps of Jesus amaze you the most and why?*

- *Consider Christ's willingness and commitment to serving others before himself. What impact does that have on you and your willingness to serve? Explain your answer.*

God the Father's Response

Philippians 2:9–11 reveals God the Father's response to all that Christ his Son accomplished. The Father exalted Christ in seven ways: (1) the Father multiplied Christ's greatness; (2) he exalted Christ's name above all names; (3) he gave Christ such great authority that one day all knees would bow before him; (4) he decreed that everyone in heaven will bow to worship Christ; (5) he declared that all demons will bow before Christ; (6) he declared that every tongue will confess Jesus Christ is Lord; and (7) as amazing as it sounds, even the Father will receive more glory and honor by sharing his throne with Christ, his Son, the God-man.[38]

Jesus' exaltation after his humiliation illustrates and proves his words that the least shall be the greatest (Mark 9:30–41; Luke 9:48). Let's examine each of these seven exaltations.

1. God exalted Christ and multiplied his greatness. In John 14:12, Jesus spoke of his followers doing greater works than he did on earth. His greatness is so magnified that through him we can do great miracles. In Matthew 18:19–20, Jesus said when two or three agree on anything in his name, God the Father will do it.

2. Jesus possesses the greatest name of all. Ever wonder why people don't bother to take the name of Buddha or other idols in vain? Those names have no power. Only the name of Christ comes with power.

3. At Jesus' name every knee will bow. One day when God allows all to know the reality of Christ as God, everyone will bow. We are told not to worship what God created. As God's Son, Jesus is worthy of worship. In the ancient world, people feared the unknown and connected their fears to imaginary gods. The reality of Jesus dispelled those fears for believers.

4. Everyone in heaven will bow to worship Christ. Believers are the people who inhabit heaven, and they are ready to worship Christ.

5. God decreed that every demonic spirit would bow to Christ. We know that on earth demons recognized Jesus and had to take orders from him. He silenced them so they would not reveal his identity (Mark 3:11–12), but in the end every demon will bow to him.

6. God decreed that every tongue will confess that Jesus Christ is Lord. Just as the soldiers who stood by the cross finally recognized Jesus as the Son of God (Mark 15:39), so all people will realize that truth.

7. Jesus brings glory and honor to God, his Father. In John 7:18, Jesus stated that he sought only the glory of God the Father. He did that through obedience all the way to his death.

• *What impresses you about these exaltations?*

- *When someone praises you, how can you give the glory to God?*

- *What causes you to honor someone?*

- *In what ways has God responded to your obedience, humility, service, and other ways you follow Christ?*

 EXPERIENCE GOD'S HEART

Reading through what Christ did and how God the Father then exalted him brings great reverence and joy to many hearts. The example of Christ reminds us to let go of our own striving and let God bless and honor us. For us, everything should be about God. For God, it is all about loving us and letting Christ show us that great love. For God, it is all about blessing us and caring for us.

- *Reread Philippians 2:6–11 and write how you experience those words in your heart.*

 SHARE GOD'S HEART

When people ask you about Jesus, remember to share all that he did for you. When you bring your testimony to a personal level of how God's love transformed your heart and life, it will likely touch others. When you also share all that Christ did, it will serve to communicate to them how much God loves them.

- *How does your Christian testimony flow from all that Christ has done for you?*

- *Write how you can weave together your personal testimony with what Christ did for all people.*

📖 THE BACKSTORY

Paul often referenced Old Testament writings without directly quoting them. Theologians call those references allusions. One of these instances appears in Philippians 2:10–11.[39] When Paul says that every knee shall bow at the name of Jesus, he draws from Isaiah 45:23 where God says, "Truly every knee will bow before me and every tongue will solemnly swear allegiance to me!"

When rabbis preached in the time of Jesus, they expected the Jewish audience to know the scriptural reference and the surrounding text. The referenced verse of Isaiah is in a passage that starts with verse 14 referring to Egypt and idols. The Jews equated Egypt with bondage.[40] The following verses leading up to Isaiah 45:23 emphasize God as the creating power of all things and the source of salvation. By alluding to that passage, Paul connects Jesus into the Godhead with the power to save people from the bondage of sin.

- *List what each verse shares that points to Jesus.*

Isaiah 45:21

Isaiah 45:22

Paul's background would have included memorizing Scriptures from childhood. Rabbis found bright students and trained them in the Scriptures and in honored Jewish traditions. Rabbi Gamaliel was Paul's teacher (Acts 22:3). Under his tutelage, Paul would have learned to memorize the entirety of Scripture and would have been tested on it. When Paul wrote Philippians, he was in prison and probably had no Scripture scrolls available to him, but he knew the Law and the Prophets so thoroughly that he could easily allude to them as well as quote them when needed.

- *How prepared are you to share the gospel without a Bible in hand or an app on your phone?*

 WORD WEALTH

Old Testament references about the glory of God provide insights into the meaning of the concept. The Hebrew word *kavod* means "glory and honor" and is used 199 times in reference to the glory of God in the Old Testament. Isaiah 6:3 mentions that God's glory permeates the universe. *Kavod* witnesses to the beauty of God and his creation.[41]

Shekinah, from the word *shachan*, means "dwelling place." *Shekinah* glory refers to the presence of God as seen in the fire by night and cloud by day that went ahead of the Israelites in the Sinai desert.[42]

- *Look up these passages that tell about when the Israelites saw God's glory and note what happened before the people saw it.*

  Leviticus 9:22–24

  Exodus 16:7

  2 Chronicles 7:1

  Ezekiel 1:22–28

Talking It Out

1. What does this portion of Philippians help you understand about Jesus as fully human and fully divine?

2. We see Christ's mindset through his choices and his focus. How does knowing this help you have the mind of Christ?

3. Paul's call for Christian unity began this passage. Unity brings peace and harmony and joy. What are you doing to bring unity to the body of believers with whom you worship and minister? What else can you do?

LESSON 5

Shine for God

(2:12–18)

Be cheerful!
Rejoice!
Speak without complaining.

You'll be a light in the world, a beacon of hope to a world that struggles and groans under brutality and divisions.

This message from Paul is about choosing joy and having a positive attitude while letting God revitalize you.

Cheerfulness is an attitude which also flows with actions that lift the spirits of others. We can sprinkle cheer into the lives of others with our deeds and our words. In Philippians 1, we read about Paul supporting actions of joy. Paul's words continue to be ones of cheer that commend his followers and remind them to choose a godly perspective.

- *What's your attitude like right now?*

- *Have you been a light to the world this week? If so, how? If not, why?*

- *What aspect of your life would you like to have revitalized?*

New Life Instructions

In Philippians 2:12, Paul opens this section of his letter with ideas to make the new life in Christ different in a great way. He picks up a thread from chapter one verse six where he expressed faith that the God who began a gracious work in his readers would continue to mature them. That means to become more developed and grown-up in the faith they profess.

Paul encourages believers to continue to make the new life in them fully manifested in their daily lives, "which brings you trembling into [God's] presence" (v. 12). Several translations use other phrases, such as "work out your own salvation with fear and trembling" (NASB). Here are some others:

- Wycliffe Bible uses "work ye with dread and trembling your health."

- The New Living Translation uses "Work hard to show the results of your salvation."

- The New Life Version says, "You must keep on working to show you have been saved from the punishment of sin."

- The Aramaic mentioned in footnote 'j' in TPT can be translated as "push through the service of your life" or "work the work of your life."

In other words, Paul is addressing believers who know Christ saved them through his death on the cross. The fact of their salvation is not in question here. Paul's focus is how to live the saved life. Salvation is ours by faith in Christ. It is God's gift, not something we earn (Ephesians 2:8–10). But once we have been justified by grace—that is, saved from the penalty of sin—we have new life to live out. That's what Paul wants us to understand. People should see our faith in Christ through how we live our daily lives and face difficulties without losing our inner joy.

- *What does it mean to you that you are saved and have a new life?*

- *How does the way you live your life show that you are saved?*

- *Now read Philippians 2:13. What does God do for us and in us as we seek to live out our new life in Christ?*

The word translated "revitalize" means "to give new life or energy." The Greek word is *energeia*. In relationship to God, it refers to his power to transition believers from point to point in his plan, and in that way accomplish progress in their lives.[43] This is a transformative energy with the power to breathe new life into us. God works within us to renew us and give us "the passion to do what pleases him" (v. 13). He does not leave us on our own. Instead, he calls on us to cooperate with him, to copartner with him, to fulfill the salvation life he has given us by his grace.

- *Read these other verses concerning renewal and jot down what they tell you is God's part and what is your part in this transformation:*

Scripture References	God's Part	Our Part
Psalm 34:18		
Psalm 51:10		
Lamentations 3:22–25		
Isaiah 40:31		
Romans 12:1–2		
2 Corinthians 4:14–18		
Colossians 3:1–10		

Grumble Free

The next few verses of Philippians 2 focus on our part in living out our salvation life.

• *Read Philippians 2:14–16. What kind of life does Paul call on us to lead?*

• *What should we eliminate from such a life?*

• *What are the positive outcomes of such a life?*

Since we live with an almighty God who promises us eternal joy, we have no reason to complain. Truly living our faith does not include putting on a fake smile and gritting our teeth as we go through the daily grind. Rather, it's about choosing to view life with God's perspective and finding the good around us so we sparkle with love.

The Greek word for "complaining" appears only a few times in the New Testament (Philippians 2:14; 1 Peter 4:9; Acts 6:1). It also translates as "murmuring" or "secret debate"—in other words, grumbling under our breath. Early Greek translators of the Old Testament used the word in reference to the Israelites' complaints to Moses as they wandered in the desert (Exodus 16:2–9; Numbers 11:1).[44]

When we complain about what we do, we're not fulfilling our responsibilities and roles with love. Instead, we are acting like children who may outwardly obey while griping under their breath, doing something, such as a chore, not from desire but because someone ordered them to. The flip side of not complaining is that instead of seeing us as grumpy people, others see us as agreeable and loving individuals, "as innocent, faultless, and pure children of God" who stand out even though we live in "the midst of a brutal and perverse culture" (Philippians 2:15). This is how we shine light into the world.

The joy that shines through ordinary days sets people apart. They glow from the inside. The constant inward peace and joy reflect a heart that knows the Lord.

- *What helps you not complain but to maintain a positive and cheerful attitude?*

- *Think of someone who always makes you smile and describe what he or she is like.*

- *Look up these verses on being a shining light and then write about the source of the light and its power:*

Matthew 5:14–16

Matthew 13:37–43

2 Corinthians 4:5–6

 EXPERIENCE GOD'S HEART

Have you found yourself grumbling lately? Perhaps you've had a tough year, or you were passed over for a promotion at work, or you feel as if God isn't answering your prayers in ways you find satisfying or beneficial. Whatever the reason, try replacing that negative approach to life with positive expressions of thanksgiving to God for his daily blessings. Start each day praising him and end it by recalling your reasons to be thankful. Remember, God loves you and has already blessed you in numerous ways. So choose gratitude and, thereby, choose joy!

- *What can you do, starting even today, to exchange grumbling for gratitude?*

❤ SHARE GOD'S HEART

When you greet someone, be sure to be encouraging. Give them a sincere compliment or ask how things have been going and offer words of cheer.

- *Commit to a week without grumbling. Choose to reframe every negative thought into something more positive. At the end of the week, reflect on your outlook and see if you are turning more to God's promise that he can use everything for good, even what is tragic or disappointing. Consider especially how your attitude influenced others. Jot down some of your observations and conclusions here.*

 THE BACKSTORY

Archeologists have dug up many remains of the ancient Philippi church. The temple, in an octagon shape, was excavated in the 1960s along with two other temples, a public bath, a baptistry, and warehouse, all from the fourth century. To the east, archaeologists found a closed courtyard surrounded by apartments that they believe housed a bishop and other clergy. These findings suggest that the church had continued to grow well after Paul's lifetime—a testimony to the love and unity of its founding.[45] The shining lights that started the church continued to produce fruit for quite a long time.

- *How are you helping your church grow?*

- *How does church growth signify that its members are living as shining lights?*

Fruitful Ministry

Paul tells us in Philippians 2:16 that his work among the believers in Philippi has not been in vain. Their fruitful lives were the evidence that his ministry had been effective. God blessed him to see these results. He knew he had done his best for God to help others know Jesus. That would be one of his reasons for rejoicing at Christ's second coming.

- *What has been the fruit of your work that gives you joy?*

- *How have you impacted lives, especially those of fellow Christians?*

A Willing Offering

In Philippians 2:17, Paul says, "I will rejoice even if my life is poured out like a liquid offering to God over your sacrificial and surrendered lives of faith." His reference to a "liquid offering" appears to hark back to the drink offering the Lord commanded in Numbers 28:7–10 and to the grain offerings in general. After a priest sacrificed an animal, he poured wine beside the altar. According to Bible scholar Merrill F. Unger, the grain offerings recognized God's sovereignty and "His bestowal of earthly blessings by dedicating to Him the best of His gifts—flour, as the main support of life; oil, the symbol of richness; wine, as the symbol of vigor and refreshment (see Ps. 104:15)."[46] Paul chose to follow God's call as an act of worship, an offering to God.

- *For more insight on the metaphor Paul uses in Philippians 2:17, read study note 'r' on this verse and record what you find there.*

Paul knew that his work for Christ could lead to the ultimate offering of his physical life. Paul was more than willing to pay this price. He invested his life in these people as an example to help them be faithful.

Fruit Takes Time

Believers do not always see the fruit of seeds they plant. The Korean church is an example of missionaries who did not see the fruit of their labors. In the 1700s, Jesuit priests introduced Christianity to the people of Peking through the study of scientific and philosophical materials. A French Jesuit baptized Yi Seung-hun, a Korean man who had come to Peking to study. He returned to South Korea and formed the first Christian community in his country. The government tried to suppress the church, but the Christian converts persevered. Authorities killed eight thousand of the community in 1866.

Starting in the mid-1800s, Protestant missionaries arrived, including two Sottish men who translated the Bible into Korean. In 1885, Korea officially allowed two missionaries from the United States to enter: a Presbyterian and a Methodist. In less than a hundred years, the church flourished, but the early missionaries saw only a glimpse of the amazing fruit of their work.

The apostle Paul also only saw small communities of Christians gather and grow, but that was enough to give him great joy. In time, those communities and many others grew so large and influential that the Roman Empire became mostly Christianized. Likewise, South Korea has become one of the biggest exporters of the Christian gospel in the contemporary world.[47]

- *Romans 12:1 encourages us to be living sacrifices as expressions of worship. This requires daily renewal to our commitment, and we must continually choose to be a sacrifice. How can you be a living sacrifice?*

• *What are you willing to do to bring others to faith in God?*

No Matter What

Paul rejoices no matter what the future holds (Philippians 2:17–18). He has no worries about his life, for his future is secure. He encourages others to celebrate with him.

When people die, we usually hold a celebration of life where we recall all the good the person did.

• *What reasons will people have to celebrate your life when you leave this earth?*

• *Like Paul, do you live a no-matter-what life? If not, what do you need to change so you can?*

Talking It Out

1. This section of Philippians 2 ends with Paul urging believers to rejoice and celebrate with ecstasy and to share their joy with him. What are you celebrating with others?

2. What can you do to sprinkle joy into the lives of people around you?

3. Paul calls on Christians to be quite different than the culture around them (2:15). How are you different from the culture in which you live? How do you stand out as a believer in Jesus Christ?

4. Paul also understood that the culture in which the Philippian believers lived was "brutal and perverse" (v. 15). How would you describe your surrounding culture? What challenges do you face as you encounter it with the life-saving message of the gospel of Christ?

LESSON 6

Living Examples

(2:19–30)

If you are part of a large family or a well-connected church community, you know how fast news can spread. When we have good news, we share it with calls, text messages, and social media posts. That encourages everyone. It's exciting to hear and share good news from family and friends, especially when it replaces sad news received in the past. We rejoice when we hear about a friend or family member who recovered from an illness or an accident, or received a job or significant accolade, or will soon experience a reunion with someone once estranged or absent.

That's the story with the news Paul shares about Timothy and Epaphroditus (Philippians 2:19–30). Both men served as shining examples of Christlikeness and spiritual maturity, who modeled all that Paul just wrote about and lived lives worthy of imitating. They were Paul's dear friends and fellow workers with him in the gospel. The Philippian Christians also cared about these men and were encouraged when either one visited them.

- *What news have you shared lately? Did your news bring joy or sorrow?*

• *Who are you excited about seeing again soon?*

Timothy's Example

Paul travelled to Lystra during his first missionary journey (Acts 14:8–30) and met Timothy there during his second missionary trek (16:1). He wanted Timothy to accompany him on the rest of his journey (v. 3).

• *Read Acts 16:1–5 when Paul first met Timothy. List facts you find about the following.*

Timothy's mother:

His father:

How believers viewed him:

What Paul realized about Timothy:

What Paul did with Timothy because of Jews in the area:

THE BACKSTORY

Circumcision began with Abraham in Genesis 17 as a sign of the covenant between Abraham, his descendants, and God.

Paul had successfully argued that gentiles did not need to be circumcised (Acts 15:1–31). And yet, he arranged for circumcision for Timothy in Philippi before adding him to his missionary team. Timothy was not required to be circumcised, but he voluntarily did it. Acts 16:3 indicates that this was done because Jews in Philippi knew of Timothy's mixed parentage. Circumcision effectively removed potential barriers between Jewish believers and Timothy.[48]

In contrast, in Galatians 2:3, Paul defended the decision that Titus did not need to be circumcised when people tried to demand it.

Timothy's name means "honoring or venerating God,"[49] and he lived up to that name.

- *Read the following passages and note Paul's words about Timothy in each one.*

  Philippians 2:19–20

  Acts 19:22

  Colossians 1:1

  Romans 16:21

  2 Corinthians 1:1

1 Thessalonians 3:2

1 Timothy 1:2

- *Read the following verses and describe how Timothy conducted himself and served as a good role model.*

  Philippians 2:22

  1 Corinthians 4:17, 16:10

  1 Thessalonians 3:6

  2 Timothy 1:3–5

  2 Timothy 3:10–11

- *Timothy was a valuable assistant to Paul and a partner in Paul's missionary work. What qualities do you value in assistants and partners?*

- *Paul mentions that, in contrast to Timothy, other people act selfishly instead of focusing on what's important to Christ (Philippians 2:21). How can you focus on what matters to Christ?*

- *Timothy matured from a believer to a leader. Have you changed roles since becoming a believer? If so, what were those changes, and how well have you handled them?*

The Example of Epaphroditus

Philippians 2:25–30 is the only section of Scripture that mentions Epaphroditus. He was more of a servant who usually stayed in the background while Timothy became a preacher and led the church at Ephesus. Paul praises Epaphroditus in these verses. Jot down what he says about this servant of Christ:

His relationship to Paul and the Philippians:

Descriptions of his ministry work:

People's feelings toward him:

His feelings toward the Philippians:

 WORD WEALTH

Apostolon is the Greek word used in 2:25 for "apostle or messenger."[50] *Leitourgon* is the word for "minister or public servant."[51] As a messenger, Epaphroditus brought an offering and news to Paul and then was sent to deliver Paul's letter to the Philippians. Paul also praised him as a minister of the gospel—someone who shares the Christian faith.

Merciful Healing

Paul writes that Epaphroditus was so ill that he nearly died, but God healed him (2:27). The illness is not named but appears to be connected to serving Paul (v. 30). He brought Paul a gift from the Philippians (4:18), which was not an easy task. Travel in those days was difficult. Sea travel meant close quarters where germs easily spread, and travel by land exposed many to the potentially deadly malaria infection.[52]

Serving God does not prevent us from experiencing serious illness or other suffering, as we see from Paul's imprisonment and Epaphroditus' life-threatening illness. But the prayers of believers and the faithfulness of God can bring miraculous healing.

Paul, who understood and used the gifts of the Holy Spirit, did not say in his letter that he expected Epaphroditus to be healed. Instead, he remarked on his joy that God showed mercy in healing Epaphroditus.

- *How have you felt when a loved one or ministry partner has been seriously ill?*

- *How has an unexpected healing or recovery impacted you?*

Compassion

Read Philippians 2:26. Note that Epaphroditus had compassion first for Paul and then for his friends in Philippi.

- *Was there a time when you felt concern for someone else while you were ill or struggling? How hard is it to think of others when you are in pain?*

- *Paul asked the Philippians (2:29) to welcome and esteem (honor) Epaphroditus because people like him deserve it. What makes a Christian worthy of honor? Can you name a few people who are worthy of honor for serving God?*

 EXPERIENCE GOD'S HEART

Paul spoke about putting others first earlier in Philippians 2. In this last section of the chapter, he praises his friends for their selfless efforts and their compassion for others. Paul was willing to send Epaphroditus back to the Philippians to bring them joy, putting the needs of these Christians above his own pleasure.

- *Describe a time when someone put you first. How did it make you feel?*

- *Is there someone in your life whom you can put first in some ways that would be meaningful to them? Who is it, and what will you do to benefit them? Even small gestures can demonstrate selfless love.*

- *How can you put your faith community before your own needs?*

❤ SHARE GOD'S HEART

Paul shared how the lives of Timothy and Epaphroditus mattered to himself and others. We want to believe that our lives are important too. So often we focus on the big things as the most important, such as bringing others to faith in Christ, leading a new ministry at church, defending the faith in a publicized debate, or visiting and caring for the elderly, sick, and poor. But actions that seem small at the time can ripple through the lives of others in meaningful and lasting ways.

My husband Jim always put people first.
He stopped to really listen to people, and
that made them feel appreciated. Toward

the end of his life, Jim still shared his faith and brought smiles to people with his sense of humor. One day he mentioned that he didn't know if he really made a difference. Within seconds, we received an email from one of his college classmates. That individual said he had been meaning to thank Jim for years. He told of a time when he had been in town, so Jim invited him to dinner. The classmate recounted how they sat down to eat, and Jim slid his napkin on his lap and then slipped into praying aloud just as easily. The prayer stayed with Jim's classmate for weeks until he decided to start praying at meals with his own family. He said that offering that simple prayer before meals changed their lives. Yes, Jim lived his life well, and even his small actions of faith impacted lives. We don't always know if our lives matter, but God does.[53]

• *Take time to share with others how their lives matter to you. Praising them also helps them know they are living well.*

- *Consider how your simple actions and casual words can make a difference. How can you be mindful to live a worthy life?*

◔ DIGGING DEEPER

Did you notice how, even when he was in prison, Paul enjoyed the community of believers? Beyond Paul's words, notice his example.

While imprisoned, Paul witnessed to soldiers and other people in authority and welcomed any to be part of the Christian community (1:12), so his ministry expanded. He received support from and stayed connected to his friends at Philippi, sharing joys and easing their worries. He had friends who were fellow workers and believers, and he realized that every day brought increases to his ministry (v. 22). Paul not only encouraged the Philippians to be united, to be comforted by Christ, to develop friendship with the Holy Spirit, to live cheerful lives, and to be shining lights, but the words he penned also revealed that unity. He pointed out the shining examples of the people with him and his feelings for his friends, all of which revealed his unselfish love and honor for them. That's quite remarkable for a believer with restricted movement and resources.

- *How do you currently live in community among friends and/or family?*

- *How do you esteem the people around you to strengthen community?*

Talking It Out

People who model the Christian faith or display a great character trait are often commended and held up as examples of how others should live. That can be great to see how to live out your faith in real life. However, it can be dangerous if you hold the person in too high esteem, forget the person is human, and fail to look more to Christ, who is perfect. When an admired person falters and sins, that can sometimes cause people to walk away from Christianity. In such situations, it's often the case that the person had become more of an idol than an example and had kept his or her flaws hidden.

Paul worked hard to live his faith, and yet he never hid his flaws. In Romans 7:15–25, he wrote about the struggle to do what is right when the flesh is weak.

1. How do you react when someone you admire fails to meet your expectations? Is it hard to forgive them?

2. How do you forgive yourself when you fail to measure up to Scripture? How do you share your flaws?

3. Do you know your own weaknesses, and do you have a strategy to remain strong in your faith in spite of the weaknesses?

4. How have you been a messenger of good news? How can you be a messenger of the good news of the gospel?

LESSON 7

Joy, Hypocrisy, and Liberating Worship

(3:1–4)

Jason Kent grew up in a Christian home, worshiped God faithfully, and served as a naval officer. Then he made a terrible decision and was sentenced to life in prison for murder. But that wasn't the end of his life. God has used Jason's life in prison as an opportunity to spread the gospel. Jason has repented of his sin and now experiences inner peace and joy in his imprisonment. He teaches Dave Ramsey's *Financial Peace* classes, is active in leadership in Evangelism Explosion, and uses other programs to connect prisoners to Christ. He is spreading the kingdom of God within prison walls.[54]

In the first century and before his conversion, Paul watched the stoning of Stephen and dragged believers to court to imprison them (Acts 7:58–8:3), and he did all of this with the legal authorization of Jewish officials committed to the destruction of the Way (9:1–3). But that wasn't the end of Paul's life. While furthering the persecution of Christians, Paul encountered Jesus and turned from prosecutor to follower, defender, evangelist, and church planter (26:1–29).

Jason Kent understands that we can have unlimited joy when we don't let our circumstances define us. He has an unshakeable and indestructible joy.

Paul starts off Philippians 3 with a return to the concept of extravagant joy based on knowing Jesus. He knows that anyone who professes Jesus may be persecuted, making it a tough choice to follow Christ. So Paul encouraged believers to look beyond their circumstances, just as he did. Throughout this chapter, Paul emphasizes what really matters above everything else, and that is Jesus.

Joy and Its Counterpart

Paul states that he doesn't mind reminding believers to be joyful. He wants them to continue to rejoice (Philippians 3:1). When we choose joy, we stop ourselves from complaining or grumbling and turn to a much better way to live.

- *Check out how biblical leaders responded to grumbling, complaining, and fear. Write down in the following chart what you find.*

Scripture	The Complainers or Fearful and Their Actions	Leaders and Their Actions
Genesis 50:15–21		
Exodus 16:1–21		

Numbers 14:1–38		
Nehemiah 5:1–13		
John 6:26–69		

- *What have you discovered in these verses about fear and grumbling and how God views such attitudes?*

- *What do these passages suggest are better ways to approach life situations?*

Beware of Hypocrites

Paul warns followers to beware of hypocrites (Philippians 3:2). The Greek word he uses as a metaphor for religious hypocrites is *kunas*, which means "dogs."[55] According to Bible scholar Fritz Rienecker:

> The Jews considered dogs to be the most despised and miserable of all creatures and used this to describe Gentiles. Perhaps it was because of the herds of dogs which prowled about eastern cities, without a home and without an owner, feeding on the refuge and filth of the streets, quarreling among themselves and attacking the passerby, that the Jews used this designation…Paul uses the term here of those who prowl around the Christian congregations, seeking to win converts.[56]

Converts to what? To the false teaching that Christ-followers "should be circumcised to please God" (v. 2).

Paul considers circumcision a chain rather than freedom and not a way to set people apart for God. Instead, he commends "heart-circumcision." This refers back to Deuteronomy 10:16 and Jeremiah 4:4 where God told people to circumcise their hearts, and

Deuteronomy 30:6 where God says he will circumcise their hearts so the people will love him. Circumcision of the heart involves cutting off the fleshy sin nature within our heart (Colossians 2:11) so we can "worship God in the power and freedom of the Holy Spirit, not in laws and religious duties" (Philippians 3:3).

- *Read Galatians 5:6 and Romans 2:26–29. What matters more than circumcision?*

- *The world often judges Christians as being hypocrites. They watch to see if we really live what we say we believe. How do you make sure you live what you believe?*

# THE EXTRA MILE

God condemned false prophets in the Old Testament (Deuteronomy 18:20; Ezekiel 13:9) as anyone who presumed to speak in his name anything that he did not command and anyone who speaks in the name of other gods. He also noted that such people offer false hope (Jeremiah 23:16–17).

The New Testament is filled with warnings about false teachers, beginning with a warning from Jesus in Matthew 24:24 that false prophets will perform great signs and wonders that deceive even true leaders. He also spoke against the false teachings of the religious leaders (16:11–12). These warnings point to both signs of error and twisting the truth.

The following chart contains Bible passages in the left-hand column. As you read each set of verses, record in the middle column what they warn against and then in the right-hand column what will happen to false teachers.

Scripture	Teaching Worthy of Warning	The Outcome of False Teaching
Matthew 7:15–20		
Matthew 23:1–33		

Acts 20:28–31		
Colossians 2:20–23		
1 Timothy 4:1–5; 6:3–6		
2 Peter 2:1–3, 9–22		
2 Peter 3:17–18		
1 John 4:1–6		

- *Based on your findings, what signs of false teaching/ teachers should you look out for?*

Worship in Spirit

- *Read John 4:21–24. What did Jesus teach about worship?*

In the same conversation with the woman at the well, Jesus said that the living water of the Holy Spirit would become a gushing fountain in believers, a spring of life. Psalm 22:3 reveals that God lives in the praises of his people. The infusion of the Spirit and praise that moves God to be active within us gives power to prayer. It's a mystery and a miracle more than something that can be taught.

- *When and how has worship moved you?*

• *Describe a time when you felt freedom or the power of God while praying?*

 EXPERIENCE GOD'S HEART

Many centuries before Paul, King Solomon prayed in the presence of the Israelites at the dedication of the Jerusalem temple (2 Chronicles 6). He blessed the people, knelt, and poured out his heart in worship. When he finished praying, fire from heaven consumed the offering and God's glory filled the temple (7:1). Let's look at Solomon's prayer as just one biblical example of what it means to humbly worship in spirit and in truth.

• *Read Solomon's prayerful worship in 2 Chronicles 6 and answer the following questions:*

In verses 4–11, what did Solomon mention about God's faithfulness?

How has God been faithful to you?

In verses 13–14, what did Solomon say about God?

How can worshiping God for his greatness remind you to trust him?

Solomon prayed for God to listen. What did he ask for God to hear and do?

– Verses 21–30

– Verses 32–33

– Verses 34–39

• *Ask God for forgiveness for your sins and the sins of those around you. As he answers, record below what he does.*

What Worship Should Not Be

In Philippians 3:3, Paul also notes that those with pure hearts of heart-circumcision will not worship merely out of a sense of duty or because of rules.

- *Jesus shared a parable of two people praying, a righteous Pharisee following laws and a sinful, humble tax collector pouring his heart out to God (Luke 18:9–14). What does this parable reveal about the two approaches to God?*

- *Which approach are you closest to when you consider your relationship to God?*

- *We can take any rule too seriously and appear intolerant and outwardly legalistic. Read what Jesus said in Luke 11:37–44 about Pharisees when they wanted to stick too tightly to the rules without love. How did Jesus regard these religious leaders? From his condemnations, what positives would you infer about how to live your life?*

Boasting in Christ or Self

- *What does Paul say about boasting in Philippians 3:3?*

Have you ever praised someone's child and seen how that touches their heart? Has anyone praised someone you love and caused you to beam? When we praise Jesus, we are praising God the Father's Son, and that pleases him. Through focusing on Christ, we also find our reason to boast is truly to praise him and to be thankful for all he does for us. He makes all the difference in our lives now and forever.

These words about boasting follow the words about hypocrites teaching that circumcision pleases God. The contrast is in the subject of our boasting. As mere humans, we are limited and have nothing to boast about in comparison to Christ. It's not empty actions, outward signs, or working to prove anything that pleases God. It's honoring his Son.

- *List several characteristics and abilities of Christ.*

- *Now list many of your own characteristics and abilities.*

- *In whom should you boast?*

Paul's Pedigree

Paul was a perfect pedigree, and he spent years building his credentials. But he realized that all he had achieved and all the acclaim he had received meant nothing compared to the greatness of Christ and what Christ did for him. As someone trained as a Pharisee, Paul used his knowledge of the Law and the Prophets to share and teach but in his Christian service to God rather than as a platform for boasting about himself.

- *How have your experiences, talents, and training become useful tools for serving Christ?*

 SHARE GOD'S HEART

Boasting about yourself has a way of alienating people and making them feel insignificant, especially if you have a strong pedigree. Boasting about God, especially testimonies of answered prayers and how he has changed you, draws people to Christ. They want to know the God who is real and changes lives.

- *How can you boast about God's work in your life to help people see his power and love?*

- *What testimonies have you heard that amazed you and inspired greater faith in you and others?*

- *What did Jesus say about worship in John 4:24? How does that impact your worship?*

- *How do you serve God when you worship?*

Talking It Out

1. Indestructible, unshakeable, unlimited joy flows from faith in Christ and what he has done for us. Each day this week think of three things God has done for you and then discuss how this affected your days.

2. Have you ever encountered false teaching in your church, a parachurch organization, or another Christian ministry? If so, what was it? How did you handle it? Would you do anything differently today? If so, what?

3. How can you and your church community avoid putting constraints of legalism on fellow Christians?

LESSON 8

The Pursuit of Transformed Living

(3:5-11)

People often want to hear others tell a bit about themselves, especially their credentials. They want to know that a person is believable and knowledgeable. It can be boring at times to listen to a long list of accomplishments, but it can also be fun to hear what others see as most important about themselves, especially when they mix what they've done with some fascinating facts. In listening to someone's Christian testimony, people want to know how God changed his or her life, and they also want to see evidence of that change.

The apostle Paul shares highlights of his pedigree, and they are quite impressive! But then he says something startling: he considers all his accomplishments, his entire resumé, as garbage (Philippians 3:8). His testimony shows how God transformed him from a persecutor of Christians to being a Christian.

We all have a past, present, and future. Transformation starts when we let go of the past and live in the present with a new focus on realizing more important future goals and moving forward with a willingness to change for the better.

No matter if your past was filled with great accomplishments, horrific tragedy, or deep-seated sin, it is the past. We are not what we once were. We are new in Christ, and we continue to experience transformation through him. Like Paul, our past becomes part of our testimony of how God has worked in our lives.

Paul's Credentials

In Philippians 3:5–6, Paul talks about his heritage, his education, and his lifestyle—all before his conversion to Jesus Christ. These are the essentials of his resumé. Let's consider what each one reveals about Paul and his past pride.

- *Read 3:5–6, and then jot down what Paul says about each of the subject areas listed below. Be sure to consult the study notes on these verses for additional insight:*

    Paul's heritage:

    Paul's education:

    Paul's lifestyle:

THE BACKSTORY

Heritage: Paul was unquestionably a Hebrew, with the blood of the patriarch Jacob flowing through his veins. His tribe's ancestry went back to Benjamin, one of Jacob's sons (Genesis 49:1–28; Romans 11:1). And the physical sign of Jewishness was circumcision, which he received "as a Jewish boy in accord with the instruction given to Abraham (Gen 17:12) and in accord with what the law later prescribed (Lev 12:3)."[57] Although Paul did nothing to earn his heritage, he took pride in it before he knew Christ.

Education: Paul's education was directed by his parents as well as his abilities and his personal drive. Acts 22:3 tells us that Paul studied under one of Israel's greatest and most respected teachers at the time, Gamaliel (5:34), who was also a Pharisee.[58] Warren Wiersbe states that "to the Jews of Paul's day, a Pharisee had reached the very summit of religious experience, the highest level a Jew could ever hope to attain."[59] The Pharisees "ruled the public life of the nation" of Israel.[60] Their spiritual authority was so great that "all acts of public worship, prayers, and sacrifices were performed according to their injunctions. Their sway over the masses was so absolute that they could obtain a hearing even when they said anything against the king or the high priest." Even the Sadducees, who held positions of power in the Jewish Sanhedrin, "adhered to the demands of the Pharisees, because otherwise the multitude would not have tolerated them."[61] Paul, then, had the best teacher and became a member of the most influential religious party in his nation. His educational credentials were impeccable.

Lifestyle: Paul's commitment to the Torah, the law of Moses, was in keeping with the Pharisees' approach to life. They "believed it was important to observe all the laws of God, which they taught were 613 in all. But they were especially known for their commitment to keep the laws of tithing and ritual purity."[62] Paul lived out his beliefs with devotion and rigorously defended them, even to the point of persecuting "the messianic believers with religious zeal" (Philippians 3:6).

- *If someone asked about your heritage, education, and lifestyle, what would you say? What stands out in each area as most important?*

Your heritage:

Your education:

Your lifestyle:

Letting Go of the Past

As great as Paul's pedigree was, in the light of Jesus Christ, he saw it differently.

• *How did Paul regard his past accomplishments as a Christian (vv. 7–8)?*

• *What did he now esteem more and why (vv. 7–8)?*

The metaphor of manure is both a negative one and a positive one. It can signify something to be thrown away as worthless. But we also know that manure can be something that helps facilitate new growth. If you live near a cow pasture and hay fields or drive by them during planting season, you can smell the manure, the waste of the animals. For farmers, the scent brings hope that the fields will fill with golden grain for cows to eat. The grain keeps cows healthy to continue to produce more milk. Manure bears fruit when it's mixed into the soil. The good thing about Paul's past that he referenced often is that it helped him share the good news of Christ and bring new hope and growth to many people. It produced spiritual fruit when he used his past experiences and knowledge to fertilize his testimony.

Paul said his past was like a pile of manure so he might be

enriched in knowing Jesus. He abandoned standing on his pedigree, but the vast knowledge of Scripture that he gained under Gamaliel also gave him a deeper understanding of the teachings and person of Jesus. Paul's experience shows that even our past can be redeemed in the service of Christ.

- *What in your past has become a testimony that brings hope to listeners?*

- *How has your transformation encouraged others to grow as Christians?*

 SHARE GOD'S HEART

Paul's self-importance had kept him from knowing Jesus. Once he let go of his own self-righteousness, he experienced Jesus, and then his testimony led others to faith in Christ.

- *Examine your own praises about yourself. How might that push people away from Christ?*

- *What can you say instead that would draw others to Christ?*

Embracing New Life

- *In Christ, what was Paul's ongoing passion (v. 9)?*

- *What is the difference between the "righteousness" one gains from law-keeping and the righteousness one receives from God? Look for details in verse 9 to answer this question.*

- *Have you ever felt righteous because of what you have done or achieved? If so, tell about it.*

- *Has your understanding of righteousness changed? If so, what is it now?*

⊘ DIGGING DEEPER

Paul contrasted his own righteousness based on keeping the Mosaic law with the righteousness that comes from God and is based on Jesus' faithfulness. The former understanding came from the Pharisees. As a Pharisee, Paul studied the Hebrew Scriptures (the Old Testament), especially the Torah. And he accepted the Pharisaic view of righteousness as obedience to the covenant that God had made with Israel. The Hebrew words (*sedeq* is the root word) related to righteousness contain the basic meaning of "right or just." The original meaning focused on conformity to a standard. God's covenant with the Hebrew people at Mount Sinai called for them to obey the law he had given them, for he was their God (Exodus 24).

Many centuries later, the prophet Ezekiel laid emphasis on righteousness as an individual action, not just as a national one (Ezekiel 18:19–32). Hosea, another prophet, proclaimed that loyalty, kindness, mercy, and turning to God rather than ritual observances are what matter to the Lord (Hosea 6:1–6; 10:12). And yet, the Pharisees reduced righteousness to a person's obedience to the Torah.[63]

Let's dig a little more deeply into this subject to see what we can learn about righteousness.

- *What is the relationship between righteousness and God?*

    Psalm 89:14

    Zephaniah 3:5

    Acts 17:31

    Hebrews 1:8–9

- *Given these passages, what do you conclude about righteousness?*

- *God's Word declared certain people righteous. Read the following passages and note the individual and reasons for calling that person righteous:*

    Genesis 6:9

    Job 1:1

    Mark 6:20

    Luke 1:5–6

    Luke 2:25

    Acts 10:22

    Hebrews 11:4

    2 Peter 2:7–8

- *Can we be right before God on our own merits? Is it a position we can achieve on our own? If not, how can we become righteous before God? Look up the following passages to answer this question:*

    Romans 4:5

    Romans 5:1–11

    Romans 9:30–10:11

    2 Corinthians 5:19–21

- *Given what you have learned about righteousness, what is your assessment of the Pharisees' view of it? Was their understanding accurate or not? Explain your answer.*

The Wonders and Power of Jesus

Paul longed to know all the wonders of Jesus (Philippians 3:10). Paul shared about the endless love of Christ (Ephesians 3:18–19) and his amazing wonders (Romans 15:18–19). Do you love to hear people's testimonies, read Bible passages, and discover something new? Do you relish talking with God in prayer? All of these are indications of the power and wonder of new life in Christ working in believers.

Paul also had a passion for the experience of the power of Christ's resurrection (Philippians 3:10). One of Paul's simplest statements of the power of the resurrection is Galatians 2:20, and because of that power, Christ lives in him. It's an incomparable power (Ephesians 1:19).

- *Paul wanted others to share his faith and passion. Read one of his prayers for others and pray the words in Ephesians 3:16–21.*

- *What wonders have you learned about Christ?*

- *What power of Christ have you experienced or seen in others?*

- *What Scriptures help you remember and pray for God's power in your life?*

The Ultimate Goal of Oneness

- *In Philippians 3:10–11, Paul talks about oneness or unity. With what or whom does he want to be united?*

- *What does this tell you about Paul's attitude toward death?*

- *Read the following passages about how the resurrection achieved power over death and jot down your findings:*

  Acts 2:22–24

  Romans 1:3–4

  1 Corinthians 15:20–23

  2 Timothy 1:9–10

  Hebrews 2:14–18

- *What are your most important conclusions about Christ's resurrection and what it accomplished?*

- *Now return to Philippians 3:10 and apply what you learned about the resurrection to Paul's comments about death, resurrection, and unity. What would you say is Paul's point?*

Along with uniting with Christ in his death and resurrection, Paul also longed to be united to him in his sufferings (3:10). Once Paul became a believer, his thoughts changed, and he discovered benefits in suffering. The apostle counted his suffering as gain, a positive aspect in his life.

- *Write the benefit(s) of suffering each of these passages mentions.*

  Romans 8:18–24

  2 Corinthians 4:7–18

  Colossians 1:24

  James 1:2–4

  1 Peter 1:5–7

♥ EXPERIENCE GOD'S HEART

Paul began Philippians 3 reminding believers never to fail to rejoice in experiencing and knowing Christ. His great focus became experiencing oneness with Christ (v. 11). Knowing Christ means to have a relationship with him. Paul's joy and peace in his circumstances illustrated his experience of the presence and love of Jesus. Paul experienced Christ through his grace, and we do, too, every time we are forgiven or blessed. Reflect on how you have experienced knowing Christ this week.

- *When have you experienced Christ's presence, and how did it impact you?*

- *What helps you know Christ better?*

Talking It Out

1. Before he knew Jesus, Paul was putting the wrong items in his ledger to account for how he measured up to God's standards. How do people still do that today?

2. For people who think they can earn their way into God's grace, what are some tactics you can use to help them see otherwise?

3. How has knowing Christ transformed your thinking?

LESSON 9

Advancing Together with Passion

(3:12–21)

Have you ever taken up a new sport? You may have found you didn't possess the right natural skills and needed to practice and to hone your body. Perhaps at first you did not have the endurance to succeed and needed to build more strength, stamina, and perseverance. We applaud great athletes for winning in their sports, knowing they put in the time to get in shape, master skills, and win. They transform their body and abilities and stay focused on their goals.

Paul compares athletic terms of one running a race to his pursuit of Christ. When he gave up his past, he realized he needed the right discipline and heart attitude for this pursuit.

- *Read the following verses and note how Paul uses the athletic imagery.*

Philippians 3:12–16

1 Corinthians 9:24–27

1 Thessalonians 2:19–20

2 Timothy 4:7–8

• *Now let's return to Philippians 3:12–16 and dig into its details. After you reread those verses, supply answers to the following questions:*

  What is the force behind Paul's strength?

  What is his focus?

  What is the prize he seeks?

  What is the unity he desires?

Consider how flabby couch potato people can be transformed when they take up jogging and make changes in their diet. The athletic imagery in this passage gives us hope that we can achieve a spiritual transformation through focus and discipline. This might mean reading and studying God's Word more, engaging in prayer, giving time to ministry, showing more care to your neighbors, spending more time serving your family, and on the list of opportunities goes. We do none of these things to try to score points with God. Instead, we do them as part of our passion to follow Christ wholeheartedly.

 EXPERIENCE GOD'S HEART

Paul urges us to be as persistent and as hard working as athletes striving to win. It takes discipline to be in shape to answer God's call. Jason Brown, the highest-paid center in the NFL, decided he needed to change after he realized that he had failed as a husband, a dad, and a believer. Jason recommitted his life and relationships to Jesus. He also chose to apply to his faith the same principles that transformed him from an overweight kid into a great football player. He called his faith discipline his "spiritual training camp." Jason's workout consisted of fasting, praying, and reading the Bible with purpose. He didn't know how to pray, so he used a book of prayers until he started praying organically. Soon he realized God was calling him to give up football and start a sweet potato farm to feed the hungry. God was with him as he switched directions and started First Fruits Farm, which has given away more than one million pounds of food. Jason and his family have also learned to live on a much smaller income. It started with discipline.[64]

- *What spiritual discipline will you commit to this week?*

Imitate Me

You may have heard fellow Christians say, "Don't follow me; follow Christ." While it's true that Jesus Christ should be our focus as we seek to love God with all we are and have (Mark 12:30; Hebrews 12:2), at the same time we need models who show us how to follow Christ well.

- *Whom did Paul say to imitate (Philippians 3:17)?*

- *Could you count yourself among those who know how to follow Christ? If not, why, and what can you do to become a model for others?*

❤ SHARE GOD'S HEART

God transformed Paul, Jason Brown, and countless others. Be open to God transforming you more. Look at changes in your life that came from God's work in you. Notice others who are transforming their lives and hearts too. It can be great to have an accountability partner where both of you commit to change.

- *How can you share with others the changes God is making in you?*

- *How can you encourage someone else who is working to change?*

Don't Imitate Them

Just as there are faithful Christians worth looking to and learning from, so there are individuals and groups who may have the veneer of spirituality but are hostile to Christ and his church. The former we should follow; the latter we should not.

- *How does Paul describe those who are against Christ? What are their characteristics (3:17–19)?*

- *How do you guard yourself from others who seem to be against Christ?*

- *What was Paul's attitude toward those who were enemies of Christ (v. 18)?*

The phrases about the lifestyle and minds of these enemies of the cross point to putting their own pleasures over eternal values and faith. The TPT study notes on 3:19 share that the Greek translation for "Their god has possessed them and made them mute" is "their god is their belly." In Aramaic, "Their boast is in their shameful lifestyles and their minds are in the dirt" is translated "their conscience is on the ground." They boast of gluttony and other sins that they should regard as shameful. Being ruled by the belly might describe overindulging in any bodily desire.[65]

Paul asks his friends to imitate his walk and that of other faithful Christians. Then he warns them about people who live by different standards. Paul mixes tears with this warning. He cares deeply about the people and understands how easily they could be led astray. He knows the dangers of following the wrong path.

- *Read 2 Timothy 2:5 about following the rules. What did Paul say happened to athletes who did otherwise?*

- *Read Hebrews 12:1–2 and list what is said about focusing on Christ.*

Paul calls people who live by different standards "enemies of the cross." In Romans 1, he provides another and fuller description of those who turn from God to go their own way.

- *Read Romans 1:18–32. Note the downward spiral that starts with turning from the truth about God. List the progressive change in the verses regarding the various areas of mind, body, and spirit.*

    Verses 21–23 (thoughts)

    Verse 24 (morality)

    Verse 25 (worship)

    Verses 26–27 (sexuality)

    Verse 28 (mindset)

    Verse 29–31 (actions)

    Verse 32 and Philippians 3:19 (the end that awaits them)

Our Identity and Future

Paul provides more encouragement for believers. He knows living in a sinful world means living with strife and struggle. He turns the focus back to Jesus and his matchless power.

- *What are we a part of even as we live on earth (Philippians 3:20)?*

- *Who is our Life-giver and what will he do for us (vv. 20–21)?*

- *What will our Life-giver accomplish through his "matchless power" (v. 21)?*

In subduing everything to himself, God demonstrates his sovereignty and reminds us that no matter how dark and evil the world gets, God is in control.

⦿ DIGGING DEEPER

Politeuma is the Greek word translated "colony" in verse 20. It can also be translated "citizenship," and it can mean either "the state, the constitution, to which as citizens we belong" or "the functions which as citizens we perform."[66] Paul's metaphor of a colony would have been clearly understood by the Philippian Christians. Their city, Philippi, was a Roman colony, and they were citizens of Rome. So they knew what it meant "to be citizens of a far-off city (even though most of them had probably never been to Rome) and they were proud of that status (Acts 16:12, 21…)."[67] Moreover, Paul's words would also have brought to mind that, as Christians, the Philippians more importantly belonged to "the city with unshakable foundations, whose architect and builder is God himself" (Hebrews 11:10). This city is the "heavenly Jerusalem above us" (Galatians 4:26), which one day will descend to earth (Revelation 21). So our citizenship is a dual one, with our highest commitment to our heavenly Lord, who is sovereign over all and in the process of bringing all things into subjection to himself. Still, our earthly citizenship matters, but it should never receive our ultimate loyalty.

⦿ WORD WEALTH

In Philippians 3:20, the Greek word translated "life-giver" is *sotera*, which can also be translated "savior." The Romans often called the emperor "savior" for conquests he made in battle. But as Christians, we know that the ultimate savior is not found in human government, the military, or in any other human institution. Our Savior is the God-man Jesus Christ, and he will one day "transform our humble bodies and transfigure us into the identical likeness of his glorified body" (v. 21).

We actually have some idea of what we will one day look like. When Jesus transfigured before some of his disciples, appearing with Moses and Elijah, the account says that even his clothes sparkled in the brightest white (Mark 9:2–7). Peter, who had seen Jesus transfigured, described the magnificence, splendor, and radiant glory of Jesus (2 Peter 1:16–18). What Peter saw was a foretaste of what even we will one day be like.

A glorified body implies the change in us when we are resurrected. After Jesus' resurrection Mary Magdalene did not recognize him until he spoke her name (John 20:11–18), and he appeared to the apostles even though they remained holed up behind locked doors (v. 26).

• *Read the following verses and record what they say about our future state.*

Romans 8:11

1 Corinthians 15:35–44

2 Corinthians 5:1–10

• *Now note what Jesus looked like and was able to do in his resurrected state.*

Luke 24:13–52

John 20:19–20, 26–27

John 21:1–14

- *Given this information, what conclusions have you drawn about our future resurrection state?*

Talking It Out

1. What is your driving goal in life? Given what Paul says about his, should you change your goal? If so, what do you think it should be?

2. What are some of the "different standards" people live by these days? Do you find them open to changing their standards? If not, why do you think that's the case?

3. What helps you realize that you are part of a colony of heaven on earth?

LESSON 10

Living in Harmony

(4:1–5)

Paul's closing to the first letter to the Thessalonians included appreciating and esteeming fellow workers, encouraging other believers, rejoicing, praying, and seeking good. His last chapter of Colossians urged believers to pray, conduct themselves wisely, and speak with grace. In this final chapter of Philippians, Paul shares how to live with joy by letting go of worry and choosing a mindset that increases joy.

Crown of Joy

Have you ever been told you bring joy or realized that someone lit up when you dropped by to visit? The person opens the door and breaks out in a huge smile, embraces you, or greets you with an excitement in their tone and words. We have the ability to brighten people's days and make their lives better when we give support and show we care. The Philippians supported Paul, and he called them his "glorious joy and crown of reward" (Philippians 4:1). "Crown" and "reward" are athletic terms. Athletes in Paul's day received a crown of laurels as their reward for victory. However, Paul's reward is intangible and everlasting.

- *Read Philippians 4:1. What words does Paul use to describe the believers in Philippi?*

- *How did Paul feel about them?*

- *What did he want them to be sure to do?*

Union with the Lord

In TPT, the footnote on the phrase "arise in the fullness of union" from verse 1 says that it is based on the Aramaic while the translation for the Greek term (*stekete*) used is "stand fast." Paul is calling on the Philippian believers to maintain their unity in the Lord, to fix their focus on God.

- *How does focusing on the Lord keep you united with other Christians?*

- *Look up these Bible passages and jot down what they say about unity.*

    Psalm 133

    Acts 1:13–14

    Acts 5:13

    1 Corinthians 1:10

    Ephesians 4:11–13

- *What are some key truths you learned about unity?*

Euodia and Syntyche

The Philippian church was not fully unified. Strife existed between two women, Euodia and Syntyche. Because Paul urges them to be "restored with one mind in our Lord," the implication is that at one time these women were united (Philippians 4:2). But Paul doesn't specify what led to the rift between them. Still, he believes the rift can be healed and harmony restored.

• *What is Paul's method for dealing with this church problem (vv. 2–3)?*

• *What else does Paul say about these women and their positive role in ministry (v. 3)?*

While urging the Philippians to live in unity, Paul reminds the believers that the two women and others have worked hard and helped spread the gospel. The Greek word for "labored" is *synathleo*, which means to share one's struggle. It's a Greek compound word. *Syn* means "to contend or compete," and *athleo* means "an athlete." As we saw in the previous chapter, the athletic imagery reflects the choice to be disciplined and work hard to reach the goal. Paul also commends a man named Clement and the rest of his fellow workers in the service of the gospel.

- *In other letters, Paul uses* synathleo *in reference to other believers who worked hard. Look these up and note his praise and appreciation for each coworker.*

  Romans 16:21

  2 Corinthians 8:23

  Colossians 4:11

  Philemon 1–2

- *When and why have you commended a faithful worker to other people?*

The Book of Life

Paul also mentions his fellow workers' names are in the "Book of Life" (Philippians 4:3). In fact, the names of all believers are in that book.

- *Look up these passages and note what they say about this book.*

   Exodus 32:31–33

   Daniel 12:1

   Malachi 3:16

   Luke 10:20

   Revelation 20:15

 EXPERIENCE GOD'S HEART

Philippians 4:1–3 calls for believers to settle any differences and be fully united. It's a call to live and work in harmony.

- *Do you need restoration with a believer? If so, how can you first begin in your heart to appreciate the other person's work and faith? What steps can you take to restore the relationship?*

- *Romans 12:18 urges us to live at peace with people. How can you befriend someone and remain at peace when you do not share the same views?*

- *What does 12:18 state about your part in living in peace with others? What can you do to maintain peace?*

❤ SHARE GOD'S HEART

The best way to get along is to share a common goal. As Christians, one of our common goals is to share the gospel. When you focus on Jesus and not individual desires, it's much easier to appreciate and love one another. Praying together is another way to connect to others through Jesus and a great activity that unites Christians.

- *How has prayer helped you unite with other Christians?*

- *What are some other things you have done to express and build commonality with fellow believers?*

- *What else do you think you can do to build and pursue common goals with the Christians near you?*

Celebrate Every Season

In Philippians 4:4–5, Paul returns to the theme of joy. We live through the natural seasons of nature that reflect the seasons of life from birth to death. We also go through other types of seasons of relationships, careers, and struggles. Paul urges us to "Be cheerful with joyous celebration in every season of life." In other words, no matter what occurs in life, we can find reason to be joyful.

• *Write the other positive attitudes Paul encourages in verses 4–5.*

• *Which of these attitudes/actions is hardest for you to do and why?*

• *Paul ends the encouragement with the reminder that the Lord is near, referring to Christ's return. How does the promise of Christ's return help you keep a positive attitude?*

 WORD WEALTH

Scripture often uses *gentleness* to describe a kind act someone does instead of taking revenge.[68] This urged Christians to live out the idea of repaying evil with good. The Greek word for "gentleness" is *epieikes*, and it also means "seemly, equitable, yielding."[69] The Aramaic word means "humility."[70] It's a heart attitude that indicates one is free from pride. It means that you are comfortable with who you are, with who God made you to be. Without pride, it's much easier to forgive, to accept criticism, and not to worry about what people say that might be offensive.

- *Read 1 Peter 3:9–17 and note below what this passage says about gentleness and humility and how to use them to repay evil with good.*

THE BACKSTORY

Paul reminds the Philippians that "our Lord is ever near" (Philippians 4:5). Paul's reference here is to Christ's second coming, not just to his continuing presence with believers.[71] Christ's words in Luke 12:36 remind Christians to always be prepared for his return.

A prayer of the early church was simply "*Maranatha!*" meaning "Our Lord, come!"[72] The book of Revelation ends with those words (22:20). And a likely second-century handbook based on the apostles' teachings uses the word at the end of a longer prayer for the Eucharist.[73]

In his commentary on Revelation, New Testament scholar Robert Mounce refers to *maranatha* as "the confession that the answers to the problems of life do not lie in man's ability to create a better world but in the return of the One whose sovereign power controls the course of human affairs."[74] We can strive for unity, but it will not be fully achieved until Jesus returns and sets all things right.

Talking It Out

1. What makes unity through Christ so different from the world's attempts to achieve peace?

2. What does your church do to help develop and maintain unity? How does it handle disunity?

3. Have you ever experienced a falling out with a fellow Christian? How did you handle it? How were your efforts received? What would you do differently if you had to go through it again?

LESSON 11

The Joy of Contentment

(4:6–13)

Betsie ten Boon spent the end of her life with her sister, Corrie, in Ravensbrück, a World War II German concentration camp. When Corrie complained about the fleas and lice in their barracks, her sister responded with gratitude for the pests. Corrie could not imagine giving thanks for fleas, but Betsie insisted that God's Word did not say to just give thanks "in pleasant circumstances." One day Betsie realized that the prison guards refused to step into their barracks because they feared the fleas. That gave Corrie and Betsy great freedom to share the gospel with the women crowded in the barracks with them. Betsie definitely lived in horrid conditions, but she still expressed great joy and refused to worry.[75]

Worry keeps us from feeling joy and being content. Worry pulls us away from trusting God and enjoying relationships. Paul addresses worry and shows how eternal optimism is the real antidote to anxieties. He reminds us to let go of worry and turn everything over to God in prayer. He also shares his secret for how to be content no matter life's circumstances.

The Alternative to Worry

- *What does Paul exhort us not to do (Philippians 4:6)?*

- *What does he tell us to do instead (vv. 6–9)? He mentions four actions for us to take:*

1. Be saturated in _____ throughout each day

2. Keep your _____ continually fixed on [what?]:

3. And fasten your thoughts on [what?]:

4. Put into practice [what?]:

ⓝ WORD WEALTH

The Greek word for "worry," *merimnate*, is also translated as "careful or anxious."[76] The Old English root word for "worry" means to "strangle or pull in different directions."[77] Studies show that worry releases stress hormones that increase the heart rate and blood pressure, cause muscles to tense, and can lead to other side effects such as ulcers, stroke, and gastric problems. Worry distracts us from trusting God, robs us of joy, and disrupts our peace of mind.

- *What causes you to worry?*

- *How do you resist anxiety?*

- *Read Matthew 6:19–34 and list what Jesus said about worry and anxiety.*

Prayer, the Healthy Antidote

Paul immediately reminds us to do more than mutter a simple prayer. We need to be "saturated in prayer" (Philippians 4:6). We need to live a prayer-filled life throughout our days. This includes a few elements of faith-filled requests and gratitude. We need to pray with the faith of knowing God is in control. This starts with praise, which reminds us that God is almighty, all-powerful, and greater than our fears and problems. It continues with offering thanks that God will take care of things. We can know that he will listen to us and that he knows us and our situations infinitely better than we do, so we have every reason to tell him all the details. We can share our day, our thoughts, our fears, our everything. And we can leave them in God's hands.

- *What has been the result when you worried and forgot to pray?*

- *What happens when you talk to God throughout the day?*

- *Read Romans 15:13. What does this reveal about peace?*

- *How does praise and looking to God's greatness lift your mind off your problems?*

Prayer's Blessings

The result of praying faithfully is a peace the world does not understand (Philippians 4:6–7). Prayer can help protect your heart and mind from all the consequences of worry. You can enjoy life and smile despite the circumstances. What a great exchange to give worry to God and receive peace in return! Dallas Willard once wrote, "Now our strategy should be one of resolute rejection of worry, while we concentrate on the future in hope and with prayer and on the past with thanksgiving."[78]

- *Read Matthew 11:28–30. What hope does Jesus give us if we give our worries to him?*

- *How has prayer been your means of hope and joy?*

Right Thinking

When we replay a worry or brood over negative words, we give our minds over to those thoughts. When we fill our minds with positive thoughts, we dwell on hope and good things. That brings peace of mind.

- *Return to Philippians 4:8. List what it says should fill our minds.*

- *Select just one or two of these items. How would these counteract worry?*

- *How might you use this approach to thinking for dealing with a situation in your life right now that has you feeling anxious? Remember to also take this matter to God in prayer.*

❤ SHARE GOD'S HEART

Unbelievers also want to think about excellence, beauty, kindness, and respect. Let those words and others in Philippians 4:8 be a bridge for talking about God with those who need him.

- *Select one or two of these concepts and pray about how you can use them with those you know who need Jesus.*

- *Now ask God to give you some opportunities to use these concepts to share your faith. Record below what you learn in the encounters.*

Praiseworthy Thinking

In the last part of verse 8, Paul speaks of dwelling or fastening our thoughts on God's works, which are always matters worthy of praise.

- *What are some of God's works that you find especially easy to praise?*

- *Consider what 1 Peter 1:6–9 says about how some of God's works can even help us deal with grief. What did you discover here that you would add to what Paul has counseled?*

Paul's Example

In Philippians 4:9, Paul once again encourages imitating his example so that "the God of peace will be with you in all things."

- *What are some teachings or practices that you have learned from Paul that you have applied or would like to apply to your life?*

- *If there's anything from Paul that you have already sought to live out, what is it? And what have been some of the fruits in your life?*

 WORD WEALTH

Paul uses many superlative words regarding God. In verse 7, he describes God's peace as transcending or surpassing understanding. That shows how hard it is to comprehend God's ability or lavish gifts.

- *Look up other superlative words Paul used to describe Christ and God the Father's love, mercy, grace, and kindness:*

    Philippians 1:2

    Philippians 1:6

    Philippians 1:7

    Philippians 1:10

    Philippians 2:9

    Philippians 3:1

    Philippians 3:10

    Romans 2:4

    2 Corinthians 8:9

    2 Corinthians 9:10

    Ephesians 5:2

Contentment

In Philippians 4:10–13, Paul reveals the source of his contentment. Let's consider what he learned.

- *What do these verses tell you about Paul's needs? What were they?*

- *What was Paul's secret for finding contentment, even in the midst of having needs?*

Paul understood needs as well as abundance. He was a victor, not a victim, because he focused on God and let his thoughts dwell on what is excellent. He did not live in denial of his situation, but he knew whom to rely on for everything.

- *When have you been really hungry but pressed on without eating?*

- *How have you responded when you have been blessed with great abundance?*

- *Is your source of strength the same as Paul's? Why or why not?*

Strength

Read verses 12–13 again. In any equation, Jesus makes the impossible possible. Christ changes the way we think and gives us the strength to do anything God wants us to accomplish. Christ changes our situation and is the One who stated that all things are possible with God (Matthew 17:20; 19:26; Mark 9:23; 10:27).

- *What does Paul explain that he trained to do?*

- *How has Christ's power strengthened you to work through struggles, especially things you might not have imagined you could do?*

EXPERIENCE GOD'S HEART

God wants to trade your worries for his peace. He wants you to share the details of your life and concerns with him. He wants you to pray more to know his presence. He wants to engage with you.

- *What worries and anxieties will you surrender to God now?*

- *How will you change the way or amount you pray?*

Talking It Out

1. How are you doing on living contentedly no matter what happens? What helps you remain content?

2. What superlative words do you use to praise God?

3. What Paul says in Philippians 4:8 does not deny the need to sometimes work through error in order to correct it. Sometimes we have to understand false views and bad behaviors so we can deal with them effectively. The biblical writers certainly didn't back away from facing off against errors of all kinds, telling the truth about them, refuting them, and replacing them with what was true, good, and beautiful. What can you do to honor what Paul says in verse 8 while also seeking to understand and respond to the many errors that seek to hurt the Christian faith and damage people's lives?

LESSON 12

The Fruit of Faithfulness

(4:14–23)

Many Christians faithfully support their local church, missionaries, and even a parachurch ministry. The people who work faithfully for Christ trust God and appreciate the support. You may receive letters of thanks that also share what's happening and provide some accountability for the money you have given. The communication between supporters and those whom we support remains important. It connects us as part of the ministry and work being done. Generous people with careers that earn money are important parts of many ministries and are called by God to share in the kingdom. In this section of Philippians 4, Paul shows how to stay in touch with and encourage those who support church ministries.

Paul expresses his appreciation for the Philippians' financial support and his assurance that God will bless them for their sacrifices and generosity. Paul learned to be content with whatever he had, leaning on God for support. He did not want money to be in the way of spreading the gospel. At the same time, he applauded generosity as well as faithfulness in giving.

He ends the letter as he began, with a message of grace. The grace that saved Paul is precious to him and something he wants believers to continually acknowledge.

Support

• *What does Paul say about the financial support he received from the Philippian church (Philippians 4:10, 14–18)? To what degree did these believers give?*

• *What did their generosity demonstrate to Paul, and how did it make him feel?*

Paul's letter to the Philippians is not the only time he talked about giving and its results. Let's consider some other passages where he brought up this subject.

- *Look up these statements Paul made about financial support and jot down what you learn:*

Scripture	Paul on Giving and Support
2 Corinthians 9:6–7	
2 Corinthians 9:11–12	
2 Corinthians 8:12	
2 Corinthians 8:14–15	
1 Timothy 6:17–19	
1 Timothy 5:17–18	
1 Corinthians 9:17–18	

- *Did you learn anything about giving that you didn't know before? If so, what?*

Sacrifices

- *Returning to Philippians 4:17–19, what did Paul expect that the Philippi believers would receive as the result of their generosity?*

Paul compares the financial gift to a sacrifice with a sweet fragrance. The Jewish offerings gave off fragrances to God. The Bible also compares our prayers to sweet fragrances rising to heaven (Revelation 5:8).

- *Look up these verses and note the comments about sacrifices and fragrances:*

    2 Corinthians 2:14–16

    Ephesians 5:1–2

    1 Peter 2:4–5

    Revelation 8:3–5

Satisfying Needs

In Philippians 4:18, Paul exclaimed, "I now have all I need—more than enough—I'm abundantly satisfied." Paul knew the difference between having his basic needs met and living in abundance. God promises to supply our needs, and at times, he'll supply even far beyond what we need. But he will not try to satisfy greed. Like a child at Christmas, we can make a long list of desires, and sometimes we can even mistake them for needs. God is not, however, our cosmic Santa Claus.

George Müller, a great man of faith, turned from a life of sin and founded schools—orphanages that cared for and educated thousands of children. He lived on trusting God to supply all his needs and those of the children under his care. Even when they appeared to be running out of milk and necessary supplies, Müller prayed and trusted God, and God always answered.[79]

♥ EXPERIENCE GOD'S HEART

Paul told the Philippians, "I am convinced that my God will fully satisfy every need you have, for I have seen the abundant riches of glory revealed to me through Jesus Christ" (v. 19). Just as God had met Paul's needs, so he would meet those of the believers in Philippi. And so he will meet ours.

- *When have you really trusted God to supply your needs? What happened?*

- *Think of your own want list. Now list what you need and cross out the things you want but don't need.*

- *Pray for your needs and thank God for how he has supplied for you in the past.*

God's Abundant Riches of Glory

Paul shared that he had seen God's rich abundance of glory (v. 19). We are also told in Scripture that God owns the cattle on a thousand hills (Psalm 50:10). This image illustrates that God's resources are limitless. When you don't get a job or make enough money to keep a house, trust that God knows your real needs and sometimes desires for you to walk through a valley. Paul trusted God in prison when he had little to nothing, and he continued to praise God. The Lord also met Paul's needs and then some.

Beside material wealth, God is rich in much more.

- *Look up these verses and list what other riches God supplies:*

  Psalm 119:72

  Romans 2:4

  Ephesians 2:4–5, 7

⊞ THE BACKSTORY

Ancient business documents used many terms that Paul borrowed to discuss generosity. The phrase "for my needs" stated the purpose of a disbursement. The "fruit" and "abundant reward" used in Philippians 4:17 are also translated as "profit or increase to your account." Increase and credit were common commercial terms in Paul's day. Ancient business accounts often involved crops and used the term *fruit*. Paul sees the believers' generosity as also bearing fruit—the fruit of an abundant reward for what they sowed. Paul uses the most common business term "I have received" for the gifts sent and then adds the language of sacrifice familiar to Jews and common in the Old Testament.[80] The switch to sacrifice returned to liturgical language and its symbolic meaning.

Paul shared his view that the Philippians' gifts were a loan that God would repay. In Romans 13:8, Paul states that the only debt a believer should owe is the debt of love. God's love for us is unlimited, so we should also be generous. That's what balances a Christians' ledger.

- *Love is the mark of a Christian. What is the evidence of love in your life?*

 SHARE GOD'S HEART

Paul shares how God will reward generosity. In Malachi 3:10 God states that he will pour out blessings on those who follow his instructions to tithe. Jesus in Luke 6:38 told his followers that God would bless them in proportion to their giving. One way to share God's love is to give others your time, talent, and money.

- *In each of those areas—time, talent, and money—how generous would you say you are, and what does your generosity look like?*

Time

Talent

Money

- *From which of these can you give even more?*

Glory and Honor

Paul again turns the focus to God (Philippians 4:20). Life is not about money. Life and everything else are all about God. God will be glorified for eternity, and we will see his glory. Revelation 19–21 make this abundantly clear.

Closing Salutations

- *Paul ends his letter with salutations (Philippians 4:20–21). Whom does he want to receive his greetings?*

- *And whose greetings does he send to the Christians in Philippi?*

Regarding the "converts from Caesar's household," recall that Paul witnessed to his jailors and everyone else he met, and this produced the fruit of conversions. These converts could have included slaves, soldiers, and paid workers. It may have also included "persons of considerable importance on the emperor's staff."[81] Whoever they were, Paul's mention of them shows that the Christian faith was making inroads to those involved in the Roman government. Christ was penetrating the household of Caesar! How incredible and glorious was that! Definitely another reason to rejoice.

• *What are the last words Paul leaves with his readers (v. 23)?*

As Bible scholar Homer Kent points out, "The realization of this benediction would increase the harmony of the congregation by causing the spirit of each believer to cherish the grace of the Lord Jesus Christ and by bringing a joyous peace among them, fulfilling the apostle's opening wish (1:2)."[82]

Talking It Out

1. How has studying Philippians changed your mindset and view of joy?

2. What other lessons have you learned from studying Philippians that will make a real difference in your Christian life?

Endnotes

1   "About The Passion Translation," *The Passion Translation: The New Testament with Psalms, Proverbs, and Song of Songs* (Savage, MN: BroadStreet Publishing Group, 2017), iv.

2   Clinton E. Arnold, Frank S. Thielman, and S. M. Baugh, *Zondervan Illustrated Bible Backgrounds Commentary: Ephesians, Philippians, Colossians, Philemon* (Grand Rapids, MI: Zondervan, 2002), 57; Ralph P. Martin, *A Hymn of Christ: Philippians 2:5–11 in Recent Interpretation and in the Setting of Early Christian Worship* (Downers Grove, IL: InterVarsity Press, 1997).

3   Oscar Cullman cites many other places where New Testament writers have included material from outside sources, including Acts 8:36–38, 1 Corinthians 8:6, 15:3–7, and Ephesians 4:4–6. See his ground-breaking book *The Earliest Christian Confessions*, trans. J. K. S. Reid, reprint ed. (Eugene, OR: Wipf & Stock, 2018; first published 1949). In his book *The Verdict of History* (Eastbourne, England: Monarch, 1988), Gary R. Habermas refers to Christological creeds which appear in part in various passages, such as Romans 1:3–4, 1 Corinthians 15:3–7, Philippians 2:6–11, 1 Timothy 3:16, and 2 Timothy 2:8. These creeds predate the letters in which they appear. (See chapter 5 of Habermas' book.)

4   G. F. Hawthorne, "Philippians, Letter to the," *Dictionary of Paul and His Letters*, ed. Gerald F. Hawthorne and Ralph P. Martin (Downers Grove, IL: InterVarsity Press, 1993), 709.

5   One resource that discusses studies of Paul's style of writing in his various letters is *Paul's Literary Style: A Stylistic and Historical Comparison of II Corinthians 11:16–12:13, Romans 8:9–39, and Philippians 3:2–4:13*, by Aida Besancon Spencer (Lanham, MD: University Press of America, 2007).

6   Merrill F. Unger, "Synagogue," *The New Unger's Bible Dictionary*, ed. R. K. Harrison (Chicago: Moody Press, 1988), 1231.

7   Unger, "Philippi," *The New Unger's Bible Dictionary*, 1002. See also Arthur A. Rupprecht, "Philippi," *The Zondervan Pictorial Encyclopedia of the Bible*, 5 vols., ed. Merrill C. Tenney (Grand Rapids, MI: Zondervan, 1976), vol. 4, 759–62.

8   Phillip J. Long, "Citizenship and Philippians," Reading Acts, October 30, 2015, https://readingacts.com/2015/10/30/citizenship-and-philippians/; Matthew Harmon, "The City of Philippi in the Bible," Bible Study Tools, accessed July 26, 2021, https://www.biblestudytools.com/blogs/matthew-s-harmon/the-city-of-philippi-in-the-bible.html.

9   Bruce F. Harris, "Philippi," *The New International Dictionary of Biblical Archaeology*, ed. Edward M. Blaiklock and R. K. Harrison (Grand Rapids, MI: Zondervan, 1983), 362.

10 Matthew Harmon, "The City of Philippi in the Bible," https://www.biblestudytools.com/blogs/matthew-s-harmon/the-city-of-philippi-in-the-bible.html.

11 Richard N. Longenecker, "The Acts of the Apostles," *The Expositor's Bible Commentary*, 12 vols., ed. Frank E. Gaebelein (Grand Rapids, MI: Zondervan, 1981), vol. 9, 458.

12 Longenecker, "The Acts of the Apostles," *The Expositor's Bible Commentary*, 223–25, 458.

13 Adriana, "Philippi Archeological Sites: The Early Christian Era," May 26, 2017, https://www.travel-zone-greece.com/blog/philippi-archaeological-sites-early-christian-era/; and Eduard Verhoef, "The Church of Philippi in the First Six Centuries of Our Era," *HTS Teologiese Studies* (2005), vol. 61, no. 1 and 2, 565–92, https://www.researchgate.net/publication/45681233_The_church_of_Philippi_in_the_first_six_centuries_of_our_era.

14 Homer A. Kent Jr., "Philippians," *The Expositor's Bible Commentary* (Grand Rapids, MI: Zondervan, 1978), vol. 11, 99.

15 Brian Simmons, "Philippians: Introduction," *The Passion Translation*, 2020 ed. (Savage, MN: BroadStreet Publishing Group, 2020), 528.

16 Simmons, "Philippians: Introduction," TPT, 529.

17 For example, see Amy Morin, "7 Scientifically Proven Benefits of Gratitude," *Psychology Today*, April 3, 2015, https://www.psychologytoday.com/us/blog/what-mentally-strong-people-dont-do/201504/7-scientifically-proven-benefits-gratitude; Imed Bouchrika, "35 Scientific Benefits of Gratitude: Mental Health Research Findings," Guide2Research, April 11, 2021, https://www.guide2research.com/research/scientific-benefits-of-gratitude.

18 Lawrence O. Richards, "Serve/Servant/Slave," *Expository Dictionary of Bible Words* (Grand Rapids, MI: Zondervan, 1985), 551–52.

19 Lesley Adkins and Roy A. Adkins, *Handbook to Life in Ancient Rome* (New York: Oxford University Press, 1994), 342.

20 Philip Keller, *A Shepherd Looks at Psalm 23* (Grand Rapids, MI: Zondervan, 1970), 116–17; Fred H. Wright, *Manners and Customs of Bible Lands* (Chicago, IL: Moody Press, 1953), 161.

21 Philippians 1:1, note 'b,' TPT.

22 Richards, "Minister/Ministry," *Expository Dictionary of Bible Words*, 443.

23 Philippians 1:1, note 'c,' TPT.

24 James Strong, *Strong's Exhaustive Concordance of the Bible* (Peabody, MA: Hendrickson, 2007), 1515.

25 Strong, *Strong's Exhaustive Concordance of the Bible*, 1506.

26 Warren Wiersbe, *Be Joyful: Even When Things Go Wrong You Can Have Joy*, 2nd ed. (Colorado Springs, CO: David C. Cook, 2008), 41.

27 Yonat Shimron, "Seminaries Partner with Prisons to Offer Inmates New Life as Ministers," *Religion News*, November 14, 2018, https://religionnews. com/2018/11/14/seminaries-partner-with-prisons-to-offer-inmates-new-life-as-ministers/.

28 Craig S. Keener, *The IVP Bible Background Commentary: New Testament*, 2nd ed. (Downers Grove, IL: InterVarsity Press, 2014), 559.

29 Strong, *Strong's Exhaustive Concordance of the Bible*, 3170.

30 Wiersbe, *Be Joyful*, 45.

31 Dallas Willard, *The Diving Conspiracy* (New York: Harper San Francisco, 1997), 293–94.

32 Karen Whiting, author, personal anecdote, January 12, 2021.

33 Derrick G. Jeter, "Doing Time in a First Century Prison," The Bible Teaching Ministry of Chuck Swindoll, July 6, 2015, https://www.insight.org/resources/ article-library/individual/doing-time-in-a-first-century-prison.

34 Jerome, as quoted by William Steuart McBirnie, *The Search for the Twelve Apostles* (Wheaton, IL: Tyndale House, 1973), 283. See also "XXIV, Death of the Apostle Paul," accessed July 3, 2021, https://www.biblestudytools.com/classics/barnes-scenes-in-life/death-of-the-apostle-paul.html.

35 Father Jim Conte was the priest in this story. He shared this experience in various sermons on multiple occasions. The sermons are unpublished, and none are dated.

36 Strong, *Strong's Exhaustive Concordance of the Bible*, 2842, 2844.

37 "Philippians, Letter to," *Dictionary of Biblical Imagery*, ed. Leland Ryken, James C. Wilhoit, and Tremper Longman III (Downers Grove, IL: InterVarsity Press, 1998), 643.

38 Philippians 2:11, note 'i,' TPT.

39 Steve Moyise, *Paul and Scripture: Studying the New Testament Use of the Old Testament* (Grand Rapids, MI: Baker Academic, 2010), 2.

40 "Egypt," *Dictionary of Biblical Imagery*, 229; see also "Ancient Jewish Education of Children and Use of Scripture," May 30, 2017, https://worldhistory.us/ ancient-history/ancient-jewish-education-of-children-and-use-of-scripture.php.

41 Matthew Richard Schlimm, *70 Words Every Christian Should Know* (Nashville, TN: Abingdon Press, 2018), 130–33.

42 Niels-Erik A. Andreasen, "Shekinah," *Dictionary of the Bible*, ed. Watson E. Mills (Macon, GA: Mercer University Press, 1990), 817.

43   Strong, *Strong's Exhaustive Concordance of the Bible*, 1753.

44   Arnold et al., *Ephesians, Philippians, Colossians, Philemon*, 58–59.

45   J. Warner Wallace, "A Brief Sample of Archeology Corroborating the Claims of the New Testament," Cold-Case Christianity with J. Warner Wallace, June 8, 2018, https://coldcasechristianity.com/writings/a-brief-sample-of-archaeology-corroborating-the-claims-of-the-new-testament/.

46   Unger, "Sacrificial Offerings," *The New Unger's Bible Dictionary*, 1107.

47   "Modern History of Korean Churches," in Yung Jae Kim, *A History of the Korean Church* (Seoul, 1992), 36–46, https://dspace.library.uu.nl/bitstream/handle/1874/605/c4.pdf.

48   *Archeological Study Bible* (Grand Rapids, MI: Zondervan, 2005), 1798, footnote.

49   Unger, "Timothy," *The New Unger's Bible Dictionary*, 1287.

50   Strong, *Strong's Exhaustive Concordance of the Bible*, 652.

51   Strong, *Strong's Exhaustive Concordance of the Bible*, 3011.

52   Arnold et al., *Ephesians, Philippians, Colossians, Philemon*, 60–61.

53   Whiting, author, personal anecdote, February 21, 2021.

54   Sherri Richards, "Mom of a Murderer: Carol Kent Shares Story of Finding Forgiveness in Midst of 'New Normal,'" *Inforum*, October 26, 2012, https://www.inforum.com/lifestyle/3032003-mom-murderer-carol-kent-shares-story-finding-forgiveness-midst-new-normal.

55   Philippians 3:2, note 'a,' TPT.

56   Fritz Rienecker, *Linguistic Key to the New Testament*, ed. Cleon L. Rogers Jr. (Grand Rapids, MI: Zondervan, 1980), 556.

57   Kent, "Philippians," *The Expositor's Bible Commentary*, 139.

58   Unger, "Gamaliel," *The New Unger's Bible Dictionary*, 454.

59   Wiersbe, *Be Joyful*, 100.

60   Unger, "Pharisees," *The New Unger's Bible Dictionary*, 998.

61   Emil Schürer, *A History of the Jewish People in the Time of Jesus Christ*, as quoted by Unger, "Pharisees," *The New Unger's Bible Dictionary*, 998.

62   *Nelson's New Illustrated Bible Dictionary*, ed. Ronald F. Youngblood (Nashville, TN: Thomas Nelson, 1995), s.v. "Pharisees."

63   Ray Sutherland, "Righteousness in the Old Testament," *Dictionary of the Bible*, 766–67.

64   Jason Brown with Paul Asay, *Centered: Trading Your Plans for a Life That Matters* (Colorado Springs, CO: Waterbrook, 2021).

65   Keener, *The IVP Bible Background Commentary*, 564.

66   Rienecker, *Linguistic Key to the New Testament*, 559.

67   Kent, "Philippians," *The Expositor's Bible Commentary*, 147.

68   Arnold et al., *Ephesians, Philippians, Colossians, Philemon*, 66.

69   Strong, *Strong's Exhaustive Concordance of the Bible*, 1933.

70   Philippians 4:5, note 'a,' TPT.

71   Keener, *The IVP Bible Background Commentary*, 565.

72   F. W. Beare, *A Commentary on The Epistle to the Philippians* (Peabody, MA: Hendrickson Publishers, 1987), 146.

73   *The Didache*, part 2, section 10.

74   Robert H. Mounce, *The Book of Revelation* (Grand Rapids, MI: William B. Eerdmans, 1977), 396.

75   Corrie ten Boon and Elizabeth and John Sherrill, *The Hiding Place* (Grand Rapids, MI: Chosen Books, 1971), 209, 220.

76   Strong, *Strong's Exhaustive Concordance of the Bible*, 3309.

77   Wiersbe, *Be Joyful*, 131.

78   Willard, *The Diving Conspiracy*, 312.

79   To learn more about George Müller, see Basil Miller, *George Müller: Man of Faith and Miracles* (Minneapolis, MN: Bethany House, 1941); George Müller, *The Autobiography of George Müller* (New Kensington, PA: Whitaker House, 1984).

80   Keener, *The IVP Bible Background Commentary*, 566.

81   Kent, "Philippians," *The Expositor's Bible Commentary*, 158.

82   Kent, "Philippians," *The Expositor's Bible Commentary*, 158–59.